GW00370462

# A MISCELLANY
#### OF
# BRITAIN

# A MISCELLANY

OF

# BRITAIN

*People* ❀ *Places* ❀ *History*
*Culture* ❀ *Customs* ❀ *Sport*

## TOM O'MEARA

ARCTURUS

ARCTURUS

Arcturus Publishing Limited
26/27 Bickels Yard
151–153 Bermondsey Street
London SE1 3HA

Published in association with
## foulsham
W. Foulsham & Co. Ltd,
The Publishing House, Bennetts Close, Cippenham,
Slough, Berkshire SL1 5AP, England

ISBN: 978-0-572-03383-5

This edition printed in 2008
Copyright © 2007 Arcturus Publishing Limited

All rights reserved

The Copyright Act prohibits (subject to certain very limited exceptions) the
making of copies of any copyright work or of a substantial part of such a work,
including the making of copies by photocopying or similar process. Written
permission to make a copy or copies must therefore normally be obtained
from the publisher in advance. It is advisable also to consult the publisher if in
any doubt as to the legality of any copying which is to be undertaken.

British Library Cataloguing-in-Publication Data: a catalogue
record for this book is available from the British Library

Printed in China

Art director: Beatriz Waller
Designer: Adelle Morris

# CONTENTS

# CONTENTS

# INTRODUCTION

'Without Britain, Europe would remain only a torso.'
**Ludwig Erhard, German politician (1897–1977)**

'Being British is about tolerance, decency and the determination
to talk about the weather on all occasions as well as a tendency,
when a stranger stands on one's foot, to apologize.'
**Martin Bell**

How do you define Britain? Encapsulating the spirit of any country is tricky, but Britain, which is made up of more than one nation and a mass of cultural idiosyncrasies and contradictions, is more difficult than most. Brits love the mix of the unpredictable and the mundane; hence the fact that, as a topic of conversation, weather is a national obsession.

It's intriguing that Brits are famed both for their manners and their bad behaviour. Outsiders laugh at the innate impulsion to queue that exists in Britain, but then cower when Brits invade their beaches during the summer months. Britain is a land where consuming copious quantities of tea is an important social convention, but Brits also binge drink and behave badly like nobody else in Europe. It may have invented the most popular sport in the world in football, but alongside it football hooliganism ranks among Britain's more infamous cultural exports.

The world's greatest writer, William Shakespeare, was a Brit and Britain boasts a long lineage of distinguished explorers, adventurers and soldiers. But its heroes tend to be complicated characters. Lord Horatio Nelson was once described as 'the greatest sailor since the world began,' but suffered all his life from seasickness. As well as being a national hero with the aura of a noble gentleman, Sir Francis Drake was a notorious pirate who built his fortune on slave trading.

And, almost nothing in Britain is entirely official: the language, the national anthem, even the constitution. It's a place where people love their pet dogs, but equally love killing foxes; a country where people enjoy a bet, but always prefer to back the underdog. In the end this book doesn't attempt to define Britain. Instead, it showcases the most interesting and illuminating of the idiosyncrasies that make up a fascinating place.

Tom O'Meara, 2007

# THIS IS BRITAIN

---

## BRITAIN'S OTHER NAMES

---

**ALBION:** *Thought to be Celtic in origin, it is an ancient name for Britain, although some argue it is more applicable to Scotland as Scotland's gaelic name is Alba. A popular term in pseudo-mythology, William Blake liked to reference Albion in his poetry, as do Pete Doherty's band Babyshambles.*
**BLIGHTY:** *A slang term for Britain, derived from the Hindu word* bilayati, *meaning foreign. It originated during the time when Britain ruled India and is still used by British expats in reference to home. 'Blighty' was particularly popular as a term during World War I when soldiers spoke of 'dear old Blighty' and prayed for a 'blighty' or wound that would take them home.*

### Doggerland

Rather than some modern-day swinger's paradise, this is the name given to the land mass which once connected Britain to mainland Europe, approximately 6,000 years ago. It joined Britain's east coast with what is now the Netherlands, Germany and Denmark and at one point was inhabited. When the ice age ended and the seas rose, Britain was born. But Doggerland still lives on in the form of Dogger Bank, a large sandbank in a shallow area of the North Sea about 100 km off the coast of England. The largest earthquake ever recorded in Britain, measuring 6.1 on the Richter scale, took place in 1931 below the sandbank forming Dogger Bank.

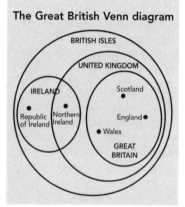

**The Great British Venn diagram**

BRITISH ISLES

UNITED KINGDOM

IRELAND

Scotland

Republic of Ireland

Northern Ireland

England

Wales

GREAT BRITAIN

## JOHN BULL

John Bull is a personification of Britain, a British version of America's Uncle Sam. But whereas Uncle Sam is an authoritarian capitalist, whose main concern appears to be military recruitment, John Bull is a down-to-earth everyman, more interested in beer, bulldogs and a quiet life. Created by the political satirist Dr John Arbuthnot in 1712, his caricature continues to strike a chord of recognition. Typically, he dresses like an English country squire in a Union Jack waistcoat and squat top hat, and is often accompanied by a bulldog. Arbuthnot gave him a sister, Peg, to represent Scotland and an arch-enemy, Louis Baboon, as a symbol of France. Neither caught on like John Bull, who admittedly is far less popular in Scotland and Wales than England.

*'One would think that in personifying itself, a nation would picture something grand, heroic and imposing, but it is characteristic of the peculiar humour of the English, and of their love of what is blunt, comic and familiar, that they have embodied their national oddities in the figure of a sturdy, corpulent old fellow.'*
American writer Washington Irving

### THE BRITISH BULLDOG

*'The nose of the bulldog has been slanted backwards so he can breathe without letting go,'* said Winston Churchill and it is due to this tenacity that the dog became a symbol of Britain. The British bulldog originated in England, with the ancestors of the modern breed used for bull baiting in the 16th and 17th centuries. This practice was banned in 1835.

*'What is crazy, loopy and un-British? Slapping a bulldog.'*
Frankie Boyle, comedian

## STIFF UPPER LIP

Thanks to the over-active tearducts of footballers like David Beckham and Paul Gascoigne and the very public displays of emotion on TV shows such as *The X-Factor*, you might be forgiven for thinking that keeping a 'stiff upper lip' is no longer a British trait. Overseas, however, the British are still regarded as a reserved, unemotional people that face misfortune with resolution and without recourse to tears. Strangely, the phrase itself, which refers to keeping a trembling lip in check, isn't British at all. It's American in origin, with its first recorded usage in the Boston newspaper, the *Massachusetts Spy*, in 1815.

### THE V-SIGN

The V-sign is a basic piece of British sign language. If the palm of the hand, below the raised and parted first and second fingers, faces outwards – as practised by Winston Churchill – it signifies victory or peace. If the back of the hand faces outwards, however, as practised by Oasis frontman Liam Gallagher, the signal roughly translates as 'f*** off'! Although the V for victory is self-explanatory, there are many theories but no consensus as to where the rude version originates from. The story that it was used by English longbow men during the Hunded Years' War to taunt the French who routinely amputated the fingers of English archers is an urban myth. The victory sign became popular during World War II when a Belgian refugee living in Britain called Victor De Lavelaye suggested that those fighting the Nazis and living in Nazi-occupied territories use it as a defiant gesture. The BBC took up the campaign, broadcasting the Morse code for V (dot-dot-dot-dash), followed by the opening bars of Beethoven's Fifth Symphony. Churchill was a great supporter of this initiative and took the opportunity to flick a V-sign, in the nicest possible way of course, whenever he could.

### Afternoon tea

As a British tradition, the taking of afternoon tea is beginning to take on the status of a myth. Although some Brits still stop work for a cup of tea and a snack around mid-afternoon, they are the exception rather than the rule. The foreign perception that at four o'clock on the dot the whole nation downs tools and sticks the kettle on before settling down for a cup of tea accompanied by a scone, slice of cake or cucumber sandwich is fairly wide of the mark.

## THE WEATHER

'*When two Englishmen meet, their first talk is of the weather,*' wrote Dr Johnson back in the 18th century. Not much has changed. Brits seem to regard talking about the weather as an ice-breaker and no doubt foreigners would suggest it's so commonplace in Britain because its inhabitants are far too reserved and emotionally stunted to just begin chatting freely without a specific reason. The weather is an excuse to start talking, but it goes deeper than that. Living in such an unpredictable climate appears to compel Brits to speculate about what the weather is going to do next, to the point where it's a national obsession.

## Why do the British drive on the left?

When the horse was king, travellers liked to keep their sword hand free to deal with hostile traffic. As most were right-handed, they kept to the left and it became the rule of the road. The Highways Bill of 1835 made it law.

### So why do other nations drive on the right?

The story goes that before the French Revolution the aristocracy drove their carriages so fast and recklessly on the left that peasants clung to the right-hand side to avoid being mown down. After the Revolution, everybody kept religiously to the right to avoid standing out from the crowd and being guillotined. Soon, the rest of Europe followed suit.

## THE DOMESDAY BOOK

Britain's first-ever census, commissioned by William the Conqueror in 1085, was a colossal task. Its aim was to work out exactly what the new king owned. In the end it listed details of more than 13,000 settlements.

*'After this had the king a large meeting, and very deep consultation with his council, about this land; how it was occupied, and by what sort of men. Then sent he his men over all England into each shire; commissioning them to find out* "How many hundreds of hides were in the shire, what land the king himself had, and what stock upon the land; or, what dues he ought to have by the year from the shire." … *So very narrowly, indeed, did he commission them to trace it out, that there was not one single hide, nor a yard of land, nay, moreover (it is shameful to tell, though he thought it no shame to do it), not even an ox, nor a cow, nor a swine was there left, that was not set down in his writ. And all the recorded particulars were afterwards brought to him.'*
Source: *The Anglo-Saxon Chronicle*, annals narrating the Anglo-Saxons' history

# NATIONAL EMBLEMS

## THE ST GEORGE'S CROSS

Officially adopted as the national flag of England during the 13th century, having previously adorned English soldiers during the Crusades, it is unclear whether or not the symbol actually predated its association with the saint in England. Overshadowed as a flag by the Union Jack for much of British history, the St George's Cross has recently enjoyed a renaissance, thanks in the main to sporting events where England competes separately. During the 2006 World Cup, 1,500,000 St George's flags were sold.

---

### The Welsh Dragon

Although the red dragon has been associated with Wales for many centuries, the Welsh flag was only granted official status in 1959. The Romans may have introduced the dragon design to Wales or it may have emerged even earlier. The green and white stripes were added by the House of Tudor during the Middle Ages. When flown, the dragon should face the flagpole. Currently, Bhutan is the only other nation in the world to have a dragon on its flag.

---

## FLAG OF SCOTLAND

Dating back to the 9th century, the Scottish flag is thought to be one of the oldest modern flags. The white cross, known as a 'saltire' represents the patron saint of Scotland, St Andrew. There has been much debate over what constitutes the correct blue for the Scottish flag and its colour has ranged from a bright sky blue to a deep navy. In 2003, following a petition to the Scottish Parliament, it was recommended that Pantone 300 blue be used as the standard hue. This is different to how the Scottish flag appears in the Union Jack, where it is Pantone 280.

The first use of the thistle as a royal symbol of Scotland was on silver coins issued by James III in 1470.

## THE THISTLE

*Legend has it that the Scots adopted the thistle as their national flower in the 13th century after a Viking invader who had removed his footwear to move more stealthily stepped on one at night. He cried out, alerting the guards of a Scottish castle to the threat. Forewarned, the Scots repelled the invaders.*

## THE ORDER OF THE THISTLE

Created in 1540 by King James V, the Order of the Thistle claims to be the second oldest order in Britain. Consisting of the King and 12 knights in imitation of Jesus Christ and the 12 apostles, its motto is *Nemo me impune lacessit*, meaning 'no-one harms me without punishment'. The modern-day equivalent would be the Scotsman in his local pub who warns strangers or enemies to 'nae mess wi me'.

### The leek and the daffodil

Both the national flower of Wales (the daffodil) and the national emblem (the leek) are traditionally worn by the Welsh on St David's Day (March 1). According to legend, Welsh soldiers were ordered to identify themselves by wearing the vegetable on their helmets in an ancient battle against the Saxons, which took place in a leek field. Although there is speculation that this story was made up by the English poet Michael Drayton, the leek has been used as a national emblem in Wales since at least 1536. Both the daffodil and the leek share the same Welsh name – *ceninen*.

A new variety of daffodil, *Narcissus 'Cardiff'*, was specially bred in 2005 to commemorate Cardiff's 50th year as the capital of Wales.

## The oak tree

The oak is an impressive tree, so it's perhaps not surprising that it is not just the national tree of England, but of Estonia, France, Germany and the US as well. In Britain the oak tree boasts an impressive and useful history. In Celtic mythology the oak was seen as a sacred tree, which provided a gateway between worlds. Nelson's ships were built of oak, as was the structure of Shakespeare's Globe Theatre. Later, oak was used not just to build houses, ships and bridges, but also as a source of charcoal. Perhaps the most famous use for an oak tree in Britain, however, was when King Charles II hid in one from Parliamentarian soldiers in 1651 following the Battle of Worcester. It is thanks to this oak tree, which stood in Boscobel Wood, that so many pubs in Britain are called 'The Royal Oak'. Other famous oaks in Britain include the Major Oak in Sherwood Forest, which is associated with Robin Hood, and the Queen Elizabeth Oak in the grounds of the Royal Palace of Hatfield in Hertfordshire, which is supposed to be where Elizabeth was told she was Queen in 1558.

*'Mighty oaks from little acorns grow.'*
British proverb

 The oldest tree in Europe is thought to be the Fortingall Yew, a yew tree in Perthshire, which is estimated to be around 4,000 years old.

## THE RED TELEPHONE BOX

The red telephone box is a symbol of Britain, which due to modernization and the growth of mobile phone usage, is fast disappearing from Britain's streets. Originally designed by Giles Gilbert Scott (who also designed Liverpool Cathedral) in the 1920s, the red booth replete with royal insignia is one of those icons like the bowler hat and Big Ben that foreigners associate with Britain. But, by the latter part of the 20th century, incessant vandalism and the persistent tendency for people to use them as urinals persuaded British Telecom to modify its approach to public telephone boxes and replace them with modern designs that are easier to maintain. There are still a few red boxes in working order and some have been given listed status, but many more have been sold off. These refurbished phone boxes, which cost between £800 and £5,000, have various new uses as shower cubicles, greenhouses, giant goldfish bowls and garden shed and bar features.

### Five facts about British telephone boxes

✳ Working red telephone boxes can be found on the Mediterranean islands of Malta and Gozo, thanks to the colonial legacy. ✳ Hollywood actor Michael Madsen, who starred in *Reservoir Dogs*, has an old British telephone box in his front garden. ✳ Australia and New Zealand once had similar telephone boxes and some have been preserved as historic sites down under. ✳ A phone box marking the spot which is supposedly the very centre of the British Isles can be found in the Lancashire village of Dunsop Bridge. ✳ Kingston upon Hull never possessed any of the iconic boxes as at one point it was the only area of the UK not under the Post Office monopoly. Instead public telephones were under the control of Hull's city council and were painted cream and had no royal insignia.

## THE KILT

There's nothing more Scottish than the kilt, but its iconic status as a national symbol is a relatively recent occurrence. It was only in the 19th century that it became associated with Scotland in this sense. A man wearing a skirt is not an exclusively Scottish phenomenon, after all, and Vikings, along with Gauls and Anglo-Saxons, all wore kilts of sorts back in ancient times. The kilt was in vogue in Scotland in the 17th and 18th centuries, but more as a fashion statement than a nationalist statement. Banning it along with other items of Highland dress in 1746 in an effort to break the power of warrior clans led some to wear it in a romantic protest. But it was in 1822, some 30 years after the ban was lifted that the kilt was elevated to the status of national symbol. When King George IV visited Scotland in 1822, the event was organized by Sir Walter Scott and kilts, tartan and Highland dress were presented in the pageantry as motifs with deep Scottish roots. Before this, the kilt was not associated with Scotland's national identity. Nowadays, the kilt is worn as part of Scotland's ceremonial dress along with a belt, jacket, sporran and, perhaps, underwear. There is no rule that states that a Scotsman should wear nothing under his kilt, but it has become a tradition of its own. Shunning underwear is known as 'going regimental' or 'military practice', so it may stem from the armed forces, but there is no official policy regarding the wearing of kilts and underwear in the Scottish military.

 Scottish soldiers wore kilts in combat during WWI, leading German troops to nickname them the *'Ladies from Hell'*.

## BAGPIPES

The bagpipes are one of the instruments that certain people hate, likening the sound to a tortured cat or a foghorn with Tourette's. But don't blame the Scots. The bagpipes may be associated more closely with Scotland than any other country, but they were most probably invented in the Middle East, with mentions in the Old Testament and Greek poetry from 400BC onwards. They almost certainly arrived in Britain with the Romans and didn't become popular in Scotland until the 12th century. Even then, they weren't seen as 'Scottish' and it wasn't until pipers began to displace harpers in the 17th and 18th centuries, and the Great Highland Bagpipe emerged, that the bagpipes came to be intertwined with Scotland's national identity. The Great Highland Bagpipe is the one most likely to be played in Scotland today.

*'No promontory town or haven of Christendom is so placed by nature and situation both to gratify friends and annoy enemies as this your Majestie's Town of Dover.'*
Walter Raleigh to Queen Elizabeth about Dover

The faces of the white cliffs of Dover erode at an average rate of 1cm per year.

## The white cliffs of Dover

Rising 350 feet high, the white cliffs of Dover are the physical face that Britain presents to continental Europe at the narrowest point of the English Channel. Known as the 'lock and key of England', before air travel, the primary route between Britain and the Continent was the crossing at Dover. The impressive white cliffs were the first thing that greeted visitors to Britain and the last thing travellers saw as they left on board ship. And, on a clear day, you can still see the coast of France from the white cliffs of Dover.

 There is a hidden network of tunnels behind the cliff face that was first created during the Middle Ages.

### '(THERE'LL BE BLUEBIRDS OVER) THE WHITE CLIFFS OF DOVER'

*'There'll be bluebirds over the white cliffs of Dover*
*Tomorrow, just you wait and see*
*There'll be love and laughter and peace ever after*
*Tomorrow when the world is free'*

Vera Lynn had a huge hit with this song during World War II. But while Lynn was born in East Ham in London, the words were written by an American, Nat Burton, who'd never even been to Dover, perhaps explaining why he imagined the unlikely sight of bluebirds circling above the cliffs.

# A POTTED TIMELINE OF BRITISH HISTORY

### Neolithic, Bronze & Iron Ages: 8300BC–AD42

**6500BC** ENGLISH CHANNEL FORMS
AND SEPARATES BRITAIN FROM
THE REST OF EUROPE

**3100BC
–1500BC** STONEHENGE BUILT DURING
THIS PERIOD

**750BC** IRON IS INTRODUCED TO BRITAIN

### Roman Britain: AD43–AD410

**AD43** ROMANS ARRIVE AND FOUND LONDINIUM (LONDON)

**AD64** BOUDICA AND HER WARRIORS BURN LONDINIUM TO THE
GROUND

**AD100** A NEW LONDINIUM IS MADE CAPITAL OF ROMAN PROVINCE OF
BRITAIN

**AD410** ROMAN ARMIES WITHDRAW

## Anglo-Saxons begin to arrive: AD410

## Anglo-Normans & Middle Ages: 1066–1347

**1066**   WILLIAM THE CONQUEROR DEFEATS KING HAROLD AT THE
BATTLE OF HASTINGS

## Late Medieval period: 1348–1484

**1348**    BUBONIC PLAGUE, OR BLACK
DEATH, INFECTS ENGLAND, QUICKLY
SPREADS TO WALES AND SCOTLAND
AND KILLS ONE THIRD OF THE
POPULATION BY THE END OF 1350

**1361**   THE PEASANTS QUITE LITERALLY
REVOLT

**1455**   THE WARS OF THE ROSES BEGIN

## Tudors & Stuarts: 1485–1713

**1517**   BRITAIN'S FIRST RECORDED
RACE RIOT BREAKS OUT IN
LONDON ON MAY DAY

**1536**   HENRY VIII EXECUTES THE
FIRST OF HIS WIVES

**1603**   QUEEN ELIZABETH I DIES

**1606**   FIRST VERSION OF THE UNION JACK IS UNVEILED

## Georgians: 1714–1836

**1770** HORATIO NELSON GOES TO SEA AT THE AGE OF 12

**1809** FIRST CURRY HOUSE OPENS IN PORTMAN SQUARE, LONDON

**1829** THE FIRST OXFORD VERSUS CAMBRIDGE BOAT RACE IS HELD

## Victorians: 1837–1900

**1837** QUEEN VICTORIA COMES TO THE THRONE

**1849** COCKFIGHTING BANNED IN ENGLAND AND WALES

**1850** THE BOWLER HAT IS INVENTED

**1858** BIG BEN IS BUILT

**1859** CHARLES DARWIN'S *ORIGIN OF SPECIES* IS PUBLISHED

**1860** FIRST FISH AND CHIP SHOP OPENS IN LONDON'S EAST END

**1879** BLACKPOOL'S ILLUMINATIONS ARE SWITCHED ON FOR THE FIRST TIME

**1884** FIRST INSTALMENT OF *THE OXFORD ENGLISH DICTIONARY* IS PUBLISHED

**1887** SHERLOCK HOLMES IS INVENTED

**1888** JACK THE RIPPER STRIKES

## Early 20th Century: 1901–1944

**1914**  WORLD WAR I BREAKS OUT

**1918** WOMEN GET THE VOTE

**1922** THE BBC IS FOUNDED

## Post-World War II: 1945–2006

**1939** WORLD WAR II BREAKS OUT

**1945** LABOUR PARTY WIN THEIR
FIRST GENERAL ELECTION

**1954** THE ROUTEMASTER BUS
IS UNVEILED

**1958** FIRST 'CARRY ON' FILM, *CARRY ON SERGEANT,* IS RELEASED

**1966** ENGLAND WIN THE WORLD CUP

**1967** BEATLES RELEASE *SGT PEPPER'S LONELY HEARTS CLUB BAND*

**1969** *MONTY PYTHON'S FLYING CIRCUS* IS BROADCAST ON TV

**1997** PRINCESS DIANA DIES

# THE GREAT BRITISH POLL

In 2002 the BBC held a poll to find out who the British public thought were the greatest Britons of all time. Canvassing 30,000 people across the country, the BBC came up with the following top 10:

| | |
|---|---|
| **1.** WINSTON CHURCHILL | **6.** ISAAC NEWTON |
| **2.** ISAMBARD KINGDOM BRUNEL | **7.** JOHN LENNON |
| **3.** PRINCESS DIANA | **8.** QUEEN ELIZABETH I |
| **4.** CHARLES DARWIN | **9.** HORATIO NELSON |
| **5.** WILLIAM SHAKESPEARE | **10.** OLIVER CROMWELL |

Below are the other 90 who made the cut. Of the 100 chosen ones, 22 were alive at the time of the poll, 14 are royals and 10 are musicians, with all the Beatles, bar Ringo, present. But it's a curious list. At least one is a Satanist (Aleister Crowley), another built a career out of opposing the British establishment (John Lydon), while yet another tried to blow up the Houses of Parliament (Guy Fawkes). Some, like Freddie Mercury, aren't strictly British. One isn't even a real person (King Arthur), while another doesn't have an identity (The Unknown Soldier). As the late DJ John Peel said at the time: *'If this list is genuine and not an elaborate Mickey-take, there is something very strange going on in our lovely country.'*

*Alfred the Great ❖ Julie Andrews ❖ David Attenborough ❖ Jane Austen ❖ Charles Babbage ❖ Robert Baden Powell ❖ Douglas Bader ❖ David Beckham ❖ Alexander Graham Bell ❖ Tony Benn ❖ Tim Berners-Lee ❖ Aneurin Bevan ❖ Tony Blair ❖ William Blake ❖ Bono ❖ William Booth ❖ Boudicca ❖ David Bowie ❖ Boy George ❖ Richard Branson ❖ Robert the Bruce ❖ Richard Burton ❖ Donald Campbell ❖ William Caxton ❖ Charlie Chaplin ❖ Geoffrey Chaucer ❖ Leonard Cheshire ❖ James Connolly ❖ Captain Cook ❖*

Michael Crawford ❖ Aleister Crowley ❖ Charles Dickens ❖ Francis Drake ❖ Edward I ❖ Edward Elgar ❖ Michael Faraday ❖ Guy Fawkes ❖ Alexander Fleming ❖ Bob Geldof ❖ Owain Glyndwr ❖ George Harrison ❖ John Harrison ❖ Stephen Hawking ❖ Henry II ❖ Henry V ❖ Henry VIII ❖ Edward Jenner ❖ King Arthur ❖ TE Lawrence ❖ David Livingstone ❖ David Lloyd George ❖ John Logie Baird ❖ John Lydon ❖ James Clerk Maxwell ❖ Paul McCartney ❖ Freddie Mercury ❖ Bernard Montgomery ❖ Bobby Moore ❖ Thomas More ❖ Eric Morecambe ❖ Florence Nightingale ❖ Thomas Paine ❖ Emmeline Pankhurst ❖ John Peel ❖ Enoch Powell ❖ Queen Elizabeth II ❖ Queen Mother ❖ Queen Victoria ❖ Walter Raleigh ❖ Steve Redgrave ❖ Richard III ❖ Cliff Richard ❖ JK Rowling ❖ Captain Scott ❖ Ernest Shackleton ❖ George Stephenson ❖ Marie Stopes ❖ Margaret Thatcher ❖ The Unknown Soldier ❖ William Tindale ❖ JRR Tolkien ❖ Alan Turing ❖ William Wallace ❖ Barnes Wallis ❖ James Watt ❖ Duke of Wellington ❖ John Wesley ❖ Frank Whittle ❖ William Wilberforce ❖ Robbie Williams.

# THE WORST BRITONS

In 2006 the BBC's *History* magazine compiled a list of the 10 'worst Britons' in history, selecting one figure from each century from the past millennium. Jack the Ripper was later voted the worst Briton of all time.

| | | | |
|---|---|---|---|
| **1900–2000:** | OSWALD MOSLEY | **1400–1500:** | THOMAS ARUNDEL |
| **1800–1900:** | JACK THE RIPPER | **1300–1400:** | HUGH DESPENSER |
| **1700–1800:** | DUKE OF CUMBERLAND | **1200–1300:** | KING JOHN |
| **1600–1700:** | TITUS OATES | **1100–1200:** | THOMAS BECKET |
| **1500–1600:** | SIR RICHARD RICH | **1000–1100:** | EADRIC STREONA |

## British celebrity timeline, from Boudicca to Beckham

CHARLES DARWIN
SIR WALTER RALEIGH
WINSTON CHURCHILL
THE BEATLES
MARGARET THATCHER
DAVID BECKHAM

BOUDICCA
KING HAROLD
WILLIAM THE CONQUEROR
HENRY VIII
QUEEN ELIZABETH I
SIR FRANCIS DRAKE
WELLINGTON

## THE BECKHAMS

There is something of a monarchist theory that if a nation doesn't have a royal couple then it will nominate or invent one. Princess Diana's death in 1997 left a vacuum, but in all honesty any romance the public harboured for Prince Charles and Princess Diana had dissipated long ago. Step forward David and Victoria Beckham. If the public could no longer have a truly royal company, then they'd adopt a pretend royal couple. And, the Beckhams were happy – no, make that desperate – to oblige. They are the standard-bearers for the cult of celebrity that is shaping and defining the 21st century. Their fame far outweighs their achievements. True, Becks was a decent footballer, but he never got close to being one of the best in the world, while Posh's career pinnacle was pouting in a flash-in-the-pan girl group. More than anything they are famous for being famous.

## SEARCH 'BECKHAM'

If you don't realize quite how famous footballer David Beckham is then take a look at Google's search statistics. There are a little over 2 million Google entries for 'Industrial Revolution', but 31.4 million for 'Beckham', which is more than 'Lennon', 'Lenin' or 'Mao', but a few million fewer than Adolf Hitler.

The latter can be overtaken, but Beckham has some way to go to beat 'Muslim' (71 million), 'Christ' (121 million) and 'God' (502 million). It's still not bad for a boy from Leytonstone.

 The American golfer, Jack Nicklaus, recently appeared on a Royal Bank of Scotland £5 note, the only living person to appear on a Scottish note besides Her Majesty the Queen and the late Queen Mother.

## BRITS TO APPEAR ON BANK NOTES

| | | | |
|---|---|---|---|
| £1 | Isaac Newton | £20 | William Shakespeare |
| £5 | Duke of Wellington | £20 | Michael Faraday |
| £5 | George Stephenson | £20 | Sir Edward Elgar |
| £5 | Elizabeth Fry | £20 | Adam Smith |
| £10 | Florence Nightingale | £50 | Sir Christopher Wren |
| £10 | Charles Dickens | £50 | Sir John Houblon |
| £10 | Charles Darwin | | |

 Economist Adam Smith, who appears on Britain's most common banknote, the £20 note, is the first Scot to be depicted on a British banknote.

# GREAT BRITISH WOMEN

## Female firsts

◆ **Boudicca,** *Queen of the Iceni people in eastern England, was the first female freedom fighter who led a major uprising against Roman occupying forces.* ◆ **Dame Stella Rimington** *became the first female Director-General of MI5 in 1992.* ◆ *Sixties icon* **Twiggy** *(born Lesley Hornby) was the first supermodel.* ◆ *Children's author* **Beatrix Potter** *was the first woman to convince children that rabbits wore jackets.* ◆ *Fashion designer and punk aristocrat* **Vivienne Westwood** *was the first woman to wear a see-through dress with no knickers to meet the Queen.* ◆ *Scottish author and campaigner* **Marie Stopes** *(1880–1958) opened the first British family planning clinic and was the first woman to try and convince men to wear condoms.* ◆ **J.K. Rowling,** *the woman behind the bestselling Harry Potter fantasy series, was the first woman to become the world's best-paid author.* ◆ **Margaret Thatcher** *was Britain's first female Prime Minister.* ◆ *Racing car driver* **Dorothy Levitt** *was the first woman to compete in a motor race in 1903. She also wrote* The Woman and the Car: A chatty little handbook for all women who motor or who want to motor.

## PRINCESS DIANA

Would Princess Diana have been seen as a great British woman if she hadn't died so tragically at the age of 36 in a car crash in Paris? Diana was a complicated figure who inspired mixed reactions. One view is of a high-profile philanthropist who supported AIDS sufferers and victims of landmines. Another is of a depressed woman, trapped in a loveless marriage who suffered from eating disorders. Diana continues to fascinate the British and a steady stream of news stories, books and TV programmes has kept her in the spotlight since her death in 1997.

## A–Z maker

Phyllis Pearsall (1906–1996) created and designed the first A to Z map of London single-handed, walking 3,000 miles in the process. The first 10,000 copies proved hard to shift. Eventually WH Smith took 250, which she delivered in a wheelbarrow. It has sold well ever since.

## THE PANKHURSTS AND THE VOTE

Emmeline Pankhurst was a founder of the British suffragette movement, along with her daughters, Christabel and Sylvia. They and like-minded women systematically campaigned for the enfranchisement of women during the early 20th century. By going on hunger strike, chaining themselves to railings and other tactics, the suffragettes put the issue firmly on the map. Following World War I, women got the vote and much of this was down to the Pankhursts.

## CALL IT VICTORIA

*According to* The Book of Lists *by David Wallechinsky and Amy Wallace, only Italian explorer Amerigo Vespucci has more square miles of the earth's surface named after him than Queen Victoria.*

Queensland *(Australia)* 666,790 ▼ Victoria *(Australia)* 227,620 ▼ Great Victoria Desert *(Australia)* 227,620 ▼ Victoria Island *(Canada)* 83,000 ▼ Lake Victoria *(Africa)* 26,000 ▼ Victoria Strait *(Canada)* 6,000

 Queen Victoria hated black, and so when she died London was decorated in purple and white to represent mourning, rather than black.

# ELIZABETH I

*'I may not be a lion, but I am a lion's cub, and I have a lion's heart.'*
Quote attributed to Elizabeth I

---

## Queen Elizabeth

The only surviving child of Henry VIII by his second queen, Anne Boleyn, Elizabeth I became queen at 25 and ruled over England and Ireland for 45 years, between 1558 and 1603. In that time Queen Elizabeth managed to avoid civil war in a troubled country, defeat the Spanish Armada, execute Mary, Queen of Scots and generally oversee the rise of England's power and influence on a global scale. But, despite many offers, she never married and never bore a successor.

---

## THE VIRGIN QUEEN?

*'I have already joined myself in marriage to a husband, namely the kingdom of England.'* So spoke Elizabeth to Parliament on the subject that would dominate her reign, confuse her councillors and captivate the nation: marriage. Throughout her reign Elizabeth strung along more than one suitor, often at the same time, frequently for political reasons. Whether she died a virgin, however, is a different matter. She was a notorious flirt and there is evidence to suggest that Elizabeth may well have entertained lovers. Before she became Queen, Elizabeth was banished from the household of Queen Dowager Katherine after an incident with her husband, Thomas Seymour. The rumour was that Katherine caught the pair in bed. Her most enduring relationship was with Robert Dudley, the Earl of Leicester, who she made her 'Master of Horse'. The common view is that she was in love with Dudley and would have married him, but couldn't due to the scandal over his previous wife's death. Many, nonetheless, believe that the relationship was consummated.

## ELIZABETH ON THE BIG SCREEN

No British monarch has attracted as much interest from film-makers as Elizabeth I. Here is a selection of films inspired by her life:

*Les Amours de la reine Élisabeth* (1912) ♦ *Mary of Scotland* (1936) ♦ *Fire Over England* (1937) ♦ *The Lion Has Wings* (1939) ♦ *The Private Lives of Elizabeth and Essex* (1939) ♦ *Young Bess* (1953) ♦ *The Virgin Queen* (1955) ♦ *The Story of Mankind* (1957) ♦ *Orlando* (1993) ♦ *Elizabeth* (1998)

### 10 NOVELS ABOUT ELIZABETH I

*Legacy* by Susan Kay * *I, Elizabeth* by Rosalind Miles * *The Virgin's Lover* by Philippa Gregory * *The Queen's Fool* by Philippa Gregory * *Queen of This Realm* by Jean Plaidy * *Virgin: Prelude to the Throne* by Robin Maxwell * *Young Bess* by Margaret Irwin * *My Enemy the Queen* by Victoria Holt * *Much Suspected of Me* by Maureen Peters * *The Queen and the Gypsy* by Constance Heaven

### QUOTES FROM ELIZABETH I

*'I know I have the body but of a weak and feeble woman; but I have the heart and stomach of a King, and of a King of England too!'*

Elizabeth's address to her troops before engagement with the Spanish Armada

\*

*'Better beggar woman and single than Queen and married.'*

Reply to the Ambassador of the Duke of Württemberg

\*

*'There is no marvel in a woman learning to speak, but there would be in teaching her to hold her tongue.'*

Elizabeth to the French Ambassador after he had praised her linguistic skills

# THE ROSE

*'O, my love's like a red, red rose'*
Robert Burns, 'A Red, Red Rose'

## AN ENGLISH FLOWER

The national flower of England appears in various patriotic guises: as a royal emblem, on the shirts of English rugby players and as the Labour Party logo. Henry VII installed the rose as a royal emblem after the civil wars between the House of Lancaster and the House of York (subsequently called the Wars of the Roses) by superimposing a red rose (symbol of Lancaster) on a white rose (symbol of York) in an attempt to bring the rival families together.

### The language of flowers

The language of flowers, or floriography, was popular in Victorian times as a means of sending coded messages via flowers and floral arrangements. In a particularly British and Victorian fashion, it was a means of expressing feelings and emotions that otherwise would not be uttered. Different coloured roses symbolized different emotions:

**Red** *love* ● **Pink** *grace, gentle feelings of love* ● **Dark Pink** *gratitude* ● **Light Pink** *admiration, sympathy* ● **White** *innocence, purity, secrecy, friendship, reverence and humility* ● **Yellow** *dying or platonic love* ● **Yellow with red tips** *friendship, falling in love* ● **Orange** *passion* ● **Burgundy** *beauty* ● **Blue** *mystery* ● **Green** *calm* ● **Black** *slavish devotion* ● **Purple** *protection, paternal/maternal love*

 As well as being England's national flower, the rose is also the national flower of the USA.

*'What's in a name? That which we call a rose
By any other name would smell as sweet.
So Romeo would, were he not Romeo call'd,
Retain that dear perfection which he owes
Without that title…'*

From William Shakespeare's *Romeo and Juliet* (1594)

---

## Rose Facts

• There are more than 30,000 varieties. It takes from 45 to 57 days to produce a market-quality rose in a greenhouse. Reasons why UK consumers buy cut flowers: 43 per cent – own use; 41 per cent – gift; 12 per cent – funeral; 4 per cent – other. Over 9 million red roses are given in the UK every Valentine's Day. They come from as far away as Chile, Kenya and India.

---

## A ROSE BY ANY OTHER NAME

Award-winning rose breeder David Austin has bred more than 190 different strains of rose since 1963 at his nursery in Shropshire. He named his first rose Constance Spry and since then has honoured many British writers, artists, landmarks and historical events by naming roses after them. Here's a selection:

*Wife of Bath ◇ Canterbury ◇ Shropshire Lass ◇ Mary Rose ◇ Alan Titchmarsh ◇ Anne Boleyn ◇ Benjamin Britten ◇ Charles Darwin ◇ Christopher Marlowe ◇ Falstaff ◇ Financial Times Centenary ◇ Jubilee Celebration ◇ Othello ◇ Portmeirion ◇ Radio Times ◇ Scarborough Fair ◇ Tess Of The d'Urbervilles ◇ The Mayflower ◇ William Shakespeare 2000 ◇ Winchester Cathedral*

# ROYAL ODDITIES

## British attitudes towards the monarchy

• 72 per cent of Brits are in favour of Britain remaining a monarchy.

• 53 per cent of Brits don't believe that Britain will still be a monarchy 100 years from now.

• 85 per cent of Brits are satisfied with the job Queen Elizabeth II is doing as monarch.

• 18 per cent of Brits believe Queen Elizabeth II should have retired when she reached 80.

• 52 per cent of Brits believe that Prince Charles will make a decent king, while 28 per cent think he'll prove a bad monarch.

• 55 per cent of Brits don't believe that Prince Charles' wife Camilla, the Duchess of Cornwall, should become Queen.

*Source: Ipsos MORI survey conducted on behalf of The Sun, 2006*

## KING GEORGE IV

King George III may have been notorious due to his bouts of madness, but his son wasn't exactly a quiet guy either. An extravagant spender and indulger, he was a whopping 17 and a half stone by the time he was 35. He liked alcohol and he liked opium and he liked sleeping with women he wasn't married to. When he married Princess Caroline of Brunswick in 1795, it was under pressure from his father, who refused to help his son out of his financial mess unless he agreed to the arranged marriage. The problem was that George was already secretly married to a commoner, Marie Anne Fitzherbert. His solution was to drink to the point where he could barely stand at his wedding. The second wedding never worked and the pair separated within the year. Taking the crown in 1821 did little to alter George IV's dissolute lifestyle and he was an unpopular monarch. His biggest legacy is the Royal Pavilion he built in Brighton.

## SANDRINGHAM TIME

King Edward VII was so fanatical about shooting that he invented a new time zone to allow him to indulge in his favourite sport for longer during the winter. He ordered that all of the clocks on the Sandringham Estate be set half an hour ahead of Greenwich Mean Time. His son George V continued the custom while he was king, but when Edward VIII came to the throne he abolished this idiosyncratic and indulgent tradition.

---

### LINE OF SUCCESSION TO THE BRITISH THRONE

**1** HRH THE PRINCE OF WALES (PRINCE CHARLES), *b.*1948, *eldest son of Queen Elizabeth II*

**2** HRH PRINCE WILLIAM OF WALES, *b.*1982, *eldest son of Prince Charles*

**3** HRH PRINCE HENRY OF WALES, *b.*1984, *youngest son of Prince Charles*

**4** HRH THE DUKE OF YORK (PRINCE ANDREW), *b.*1960, *second son of Queen Elizabeth II*

**5** HRH PRINCESS BEATRICE OF YORK, *b.*1988, *eldest daughter of the Duke of York*

**6** HRH PRINCESS EUGENIE OF YORK, *b.*1990, *youngest daughter of the Duke of York*

**7** HRH THE EARL OF WESSEX (PRINCE EDWARD), *b.*1964, *third son of Queen Elizabeth II*

**8** LADY LOUISE WINDSOR, *b.*2003, *daughter of the Earl of Wessex*

**9** HRH THE PRINCESS ROYAL (PRINCESS ANNE), *b.*1950, *daughter of Queen Elizabeth II*

**10** PETER PHILLIPS, *b.*1977, *son of the Princess Royal*

**11** ZARA PHILLIPS, *b.*1981, *daughter of the Princess Royal*

**12** DAVID ARMSTRONG-JONES, VISCOUNT LINLEY, *b.*1961, *grandson of King George VI through his daughter Princess Margaret*

**13** THE HON. CHARLES ARMSTRONG-JONES, *b.*1999, *son of Viscount Linley*

**14** THE HON. MARGARITA ARMSTRONG-JONES, *b.*2002, *daughter of Viscount Linley*

**15** LADY SARAH CHATTO, *b.*1964, *grand-daughter of King George VI*

## Monarchs of England

HOUSE OF WESSEX

| | |
|---|---|
| Egbert | 802–839 |
| Ethelwulf | 839–856 |
| Aethelbald | 856–860 |
| Aethelbert | 860–866 |
| Aethelred | 866–871 |
| Alfred the Great | 871–899 |
| Edward the Elder | 899–925 |
| Athelstan | 925–940 |
| Edmund the Magnificent | 940–946 |
| Eadred | 946–955 |
| Eadwig (Edwy) All-Fair | 955–959 |
| Edgar the Peaceable | 959–975 |
| Edward the Martyr | 975–978 |
| Æthelred II | 978–1016 |
| (Ethelred the Unready) | |
| Edmund II (Ironside) | 1016 |

DANISH

| | |
|---|---|
| Svein Forkbeard | 1014 |

| | |
|---|---|
| Cnut (Canute) | 1016–1035 |
| Harold I | 1035–1040 |
| Hardicnut | 1040–1042 |

SAXONS

| | |
|---|---|
| Edward (the Confessor) | 1042–1066 |
| Harold II | 1066 |

NORMANS

| | |
|---|---|
| William I | 1066–1087 |
| William II | 1087–1100 |
| Henry I | 1100–1135 |
| Stephen | 1135–1154 |

PLANTAGENETS

| | |
|---|---|
| Henry II | 1154–1189 |
| Richard I | 1189–1199 |
| John | 1199–1216 |
| Henry III | 1216–1272 |
| Edward I | 1272–1307 |
| Edward II | 1307–1327 |
| Edward III | 1327–1377 |
| Richard II | 1377–1399 |

HOUSE OF LANCASTER

| | |
|---|---|
| Henry IV | 1399–1413 |
| Henry V | 1413–1422 |
| Henry VI | 1422–1461 |

| James II | 1685–1688 |
| William III | 1689–1702 |
| Mary II | 1689–1694 |
| Anne | 1702–1714 |

HOUSE OF HANOVER

| George I | 1714–1727 |
| George II | 1727–1760 |
| George III | 1760–1820 |
| George IV | 1820–1830 |
| William IV | 1830–1837 |
| Victoria | 1837–1901 |

HOUSE OF YORK

| Edward IV | 1461–1483 |
| Edward V | 1483 |
| Richard III | 1483–1485 |

SAXE-COBURG-GOTHA

| Edward VII | 1901–1910 |

TUDORS

| Henry VII | 1485–1509 |
| Henry VIII | 1509–1547 |
| Edward VI | 1547–1553 |
| Jane Grey | 1553 |
| Mary I | 1553–1558 |
| Elizabeth I | 1558–1603 |

WINDSOR

| George V | 1910–1936 |
| Edward VIII | 1936–1936 |
| George VI | 1936–1952 |
| Elizabeth II | 1952–present |

STUARTS

| James I | 1603–1625 |
| Charles I | 1625–1649 |

COMMONWEALTH

| Oliver Cromwell | 1649–1658 |
| Richard Cromwell | 1658–1659 |

STUARTS (RESTORED)

| Charles II | 1660–1685 |

# HENRY VIII

*'If a lion knew his strength, it were hard for any man to hold him.'*
Sir Thomas More on Henry VIII

## HENRY VIII

Born 28 June 1491 in Greenwich Palace, Britain's most notorious monarch, Henry VIII, was not yet 18 when he came to the throne. He never expected to become king: the succession only passed to him when his elder brother, Arthur, died. It wasn't just the right to the throne he inherited, he also acquired his brother's wife, Catherine of Aragon. She was to be the first of many. Henry switched wives like some modern men trade in cars and, although many of his actions were hugely significant in terms of the relationship between church and state, it is for this ferocious appetite in wives that he is more renowned than for anything else. Henry died in 1547: like an early, English incarnation of Elvis, his former glory fading, he was grossly overweight, played out and quite probably suffering from syphilis.

### Exactly how many wives did Henry VIII have?

The popular conception is that Henry VIII had six wives, their fates recorded by the mnemonic: 'divorced, beheaded, died, divorced, beheaded, survived'. Henry's voracious appetite for spouses was not so much driven by his libido (although that undoubtedly played a part), but by his desire to sire a male successor. But some argue that since four of Henry's marriages ended in annulments rather than divorce, which means that legally the marriages never actually took place, he was only actually married twice – to Jane Seymour, who died following childbirth and Catherine Parr, who outlived him.

## THE BOLEYN SISTERS

Of all Henry's women, Anne Boleyn is the one who has captivated the public imagination the most. Rumoured to possess six fingers, an extra nipple and a large mole or goiter on her neck, she was even thought by some to be a witch. Born in 1500 and married to Henry in 1533, she was just 36 when she was beheaded three years later on charges of adultery, incest and plotting to kill the king. But Anne's elder sister, Mary, also led a lively life, which intertwined with that of Henry VIII. Prior to marrying Anne, Henry had an affair with Mary, who was married to William Carey. According to one source, a member of Parliament attacked the king's morals in 1528 and accused Henry of sleeping with both Anne's mother and sister. *'Never with her mother,'* he allegedly replied. In 1526, Mary had a child, Henry Carey, who could well have been the bastard son of Henry VIII. Before her relationship with Henry, while living in France, Mary was also supposed to have had an affair with the French King, Francis I, who reputedly referred to her as *'my English mare'* and retrospectively described her as *'a great whore, the most infamous of all'*.

### Henry's naval legacy

Henry VIII invested heavily in the navy, which grew from three to 53 ships during his reign. The remains of one of these vessels, the *Mary Rose,* now resides in Portsmouth Naval Museum. Without the naval expansion driven by Henry, it is unlikely England would have beaten the Spanish Armada during the reign of Elizabeth I, nor set up the overseas colonies that became the foundation for the British Empire.

 Although Henry VIII was an accomplished musician and wrote a number of pieces of music, the idea that he composed the melody to 'Greensleeves' as some sort of ode to Anne Boleyn is a popular myth.

# THE CURRENT QUEEN

## A day in the working life of the Queen

**MORNINGS** Scans the daily newspapers. Reviews a selection of her correspondence (the Queen receives 200–300 letters from the public a day). Deals with official papers and documents with two of her private secretaries. Process normally takes an hour. Takes official meetings or 'audiences' with ambassadors, high commissioners, bishops, judges and national award-winners. Each meeting lasts 10 to 20 minutes. If scheduled, ceremonies for the presentation of honours and decorations known as investitures take place at 11 am and last for just over an hour. The Queen will typically meet around 100 people at each investiture.

**LUNCH** If at home, the Queen will lunch privately, although every few months she and the Duke of Edinburgh will invite a dozen guests from a wide variety of backgrounds to an informal lunch. If on a regional visit, the Queen and the Duke of Edinburgh lunch with a variety of people in venues ranging from town halls to hospitals.

**AFTERNOONS** The Queen tends to spend afternoons fulfilling public engagements. She carries out around 430 engagements a year, which involve meeting people, opening events and buildings, unveiling plaques and making speeches. If there's time the Queen will end the afternoon by seeing a number of government ministers in a meeting of the Privy Council.

**EVENINGS** Every Wednesday at 6.30 pm the Queen meets the Prime Minister for a private summit if they are both in London. At 7.30 pm a report of the day's parliamentary proceedings, written by one of the government's whips, arrives and the Queen reads it. On some evenings the Queen may attend a film première, a concert performance in aid of a charitable cause, or a reception linked to organizations of which she is patron. She also regularly hosts official receptions at Buckingham Palace.

 The only house in England that the Queen may not enter is the House of Commons as she is not a commoner.

Her Majesty has owned more than 30 corgis during her reign. The first, called Susan, was a present on her 18th birthday in 1944.

## Incidents that made the headlines

● In July 1982, the Queen woke to find 31-year-old Michael Fagan bleeding all over the royal bed linen. The Queen rang the police, but they never came. The gatecrasher had planned to commit suicide in the royal bedroom, but in the end decided it 'wasn't a nice thing to do'.

● In 2005, Al-Qaida named the Queen 'one of the severest enemies of Islam'.

● In December 2003, one of the Queen's corgis, Pharos, was killed after being mauled by Princess Anne's bull terrier, Dotty. A year before, Princess Anne became the first member of the royal family to have a criminal record when she admitted a charge under the Dangerous Dogs Act after Dotty had bitten two children in Windsor Great Park.

---

### STAMP OF AUTHORITY

*The Queen has been depicted on the banknotes of 33 issuing authorities. The countries and issuing authorities that have used portraits of the Queen are (in alphabetical order):*

Australia ✳ Bahamas ✳ Belize ✳ Bermuda ✳ British Caribbean Territories ✳ British Honduras ✳ Canada ✳ Cayman Islands ✳ Ceylon ✳ Cyprus ✳ East African Currency Board ✳ East Caribbean States ✳ Falkland Islands ✳ Fiji ✳ Gibraltar ✳ Great Britain (Bank of England) ✳ Guernsey ✳ Hong Kong ✳ Isle of Man ✳ Jamaica ✳ Jersey ✳ Malaya and North Borneo ✳ Malta ✳ Mauritius ✳ New Zealand ✳ Rhodesia and Nyasaland ✳ Rhodesia ✳ Saint Helena ✳ Scotland (Royal Bank of Scotland) ✳ Seychelles ✳ Solomon Islands ✳ Southern Rhodesia ✳ Trinidad and Tobago

# PRIME MINISTERS

Originally a term of abuse, the first official *'Prime Minister'* was Sir Henry Campbell-Bannerman in 1905. Although Benjamin Disraeli used the title in official documents, prior to this the official title of the person we now call the Prime Minister was First Lord of the Treasury.

**1721–42** Sir Robert Walpole WHIG

**1742–3** Spencer Compton, *Earl of Wilmington* WHIG

**1743–54** Henry Pelham WHIG

**1754–6** Thomas Pelham-Holles, *Duke of Newcastle* WHIG

**1756–7** William Cavendish, *Duke of Devonshire* WHIG

**1757–62** Thomas Pelham-Holles, *Duke of Newcastle* WHIG

**1762–3** John Stuart, *Earl of Bute* TORY

**1763–5** George Grenville WHIG

**1765–6, 1782** Charles Wentworth, *Marquess of Rockingham* WHIG

**1766–8** The Earl of Chatham, William Pitt *'The Elder'* WHIG

**1768–70** Augustus Henry Fitzroy, *Duke of Grafton* WHIG

**1770–82** Frederick North, *Lord North* TORY

**1782–3** William Petty, *Earl of Shelburne* WHIG

**1783** William Bentinck, *Duke of Portland* WHIG

**1783–1801** William Pitt *'The Younger'* TORY

**1801–4** Henry Addington TORY

**1804–6** William Pitt *'The Younger'* TORY

**1806–7** William Wyndam Grenville, *Lord Grenville* WHIG

**1807–9** William Bentinck, *Duke of Portland* WHIG

**1809–12** Spencer Perceval TORY

**1812–27** Robert Banks Jenkinson, *Earl of Liverpool* TORY

**1827** George Canning TORY

**1827–8** Frederick Robinson, *Viscount Goderich* TORY

**1828–30** Arthur Wellesley, *Duke of Wellington* TORY

**1830–34** Charles Grey, *Earl Grey* WHIG

**1834** William Lamb, *Viscount Melbourne* WHIG

**1834–5** Sir Robert Peel TORY

**1835–41** William Lamb, *Viscount Melbourne* WHIG

**1841–6** Sir Robert Peel TORY

**1846–51** John Russell, *Earl Russell* LIBERAL

**1852** Edward Stanley, *Earl of Derby* CONSERVATIVE

**1852–5** George Hamilton-Gordon, *Earl of Aberdeen* CONSERVATIVE

**1855–8** Henry Temple, *Viscount Palmerston* LIBERAL

**1858–9** Edward Stanley, *Earl of Derby* CONSERVATIVE

**1859–65** Henry Temple, *Viscount Palmerston* LIBERAL

**1865–6** John Russell, *Earl Russell* LIBERAL

**1866–8** Edward Stanley, *Earl of Derby* CONSERVATIVE

**1868** Benjamin Disraeli CONSERVATIVE

**1868–74** William Gladstone LIBERAL

**1874–80** Benjamin Disraeli CONSERVATIVE

**1880–85** William Gladstone LIBERAL

**1885–6** Robert Gascoyne-Cecil, *Marquess of Salisbury* CONSERVATIVE

**1886** William Gladstone LIBERAL

**1886–92** Robert Gascoyne-Cecil, *Marquess of Salisbury* CONSERVATIVE

**1892–94** William Gladstone LIBERAL

**1894–5** Philip Archibald, *Earl of Rosebery* LIBERAL

**1895–1902** Robert Gascoyne-Cecil, *Marquess of Salisbury* CONSERVATIVE

**1902–5** James Balfour CONSERVATIVE

**1905–8** Henry Campbell-Bannerman LIBERAL

**1908–16** Herbert Henry Asquith LIBERAL

**1916–22** David Lloyd George LIBERAL

**1922–3** Andrew Bonar Law CONSERVATIVE

**1923** Stanley Baldwin CONSERVATIVE

**1924** James Ramsay MacDonald LABOUR

**1924–9** Stanley Baldwin CONSERVATIVE

**1929–35** James Ramsay MacDonald LABOUR

**1935–7** Stanley Baldwin CONSERVATIVE

**1937–40** Arthur Neville Chamberlain CONSERVATIVE

**1940–5** Sir Winston Leonard Spencer Churchill CONSERVATIVE

**1945–51** Clement Richard Attlee LABOUR

**1951–5** Sir Winston Leonard Spencer Churchill CONSERVATIVE

**1955–7** Anthony Eden CONSERVATIVE

**1957–63** Harold Macmillan CONSERVATIVE

**1963–4** Sir Alec Douglas-Home CONSERVATIVE

**1964–70** Harold Wilson LABOUR

**1970–4** Edward Heath CONSERVATIVE

**1974–6** Harold Wilson LABOUR

**1976–9** James Callaghan LABOUR

**1979–90** Margaret Thatcher CONSERVATIVE

**1990–97** John Major CONSERVATIVE

**1997–2007** Tony Blair LABOUR

**2007–** Gordon Brown LABOUR

# WINSTON CHURCHILL

*'We shall defend our island, whatever the cost may be, we shall fight on the beaches, we shall fight on the landing grounds, we shall fight in the fields and in the streets, we shall fight in the hills; we shall never surrender.'*

Winston Churchill

## 11 things you may not know about Winston Churchill

♦ *Churchill's actual surname was Spencer-Churchill.* ♦ Winston Churchill was the school fencing champion at Harrow. ♦ *It took Churchill three attempts to get into the Royal Military Academy, Sandhurst.* ♦ He won the Nobel Prize for literature in 1953. ♦ *Churchill had a mild heart attack in December 1941 while visiting the White House.* ♦ Churchill suffered from depression, which he called the 'black dog'. ♦ *He also suffered from a lisp.* ♦ According to a Gallup poll conducted in the US, Winston Churchill was the 10th-most-admired person of the 20th century. ♦ *In 1965 Churchill became the first person other than a monarch to appear on a British coin.* ♦ Churchill was half-American by birth. ♦ *Churchill suffered a stroke and died on 24 January 1965, 70 years to the day after his father's death.*

### WINSTON CHURCHILL'S TEETH

Churchill's teeth gave him considerable trouble in his youth and by the time he was governing Britain during World War II he wore dentures. These were custom-made by dentist Wilfred Fish to leave a gap between the plate and roof of his mouth to accommodate his natural lisp and not detract from his distinctive speaking style. Churchill's spare set of dentures resides in the Royal College of Surgeons museum, England.

## SOME FAMOUS QUOTES

'I have nothing to offer but blood, toil, tears, and sweat.'

✳

'If the British Empire and its Commonwealth last a thousand years, men will still say, "This was their finest hour."'

✳

'Never in the field of human conflict was so much owed by so many to so few.' [about the Battle of Britain pilots]

✳

'This is not the end. It is not even the beginning of the end. But it is, perhaps, the end of the beginning.'

✳

'Courage is what it takes to stand up and speak; courage is also what it takes to sit down and listen.'

✳

'We shall fight on the beaches, we shall fight on the landing grounds, we shall fight in the fields and in the streets, we shall fight in the hills; we shall never surrender.'

## THE IRON CURTAIN

Although the term the Iron Curtain, used to define the division between western Europe and the Soviet Union, was coined by Nazi propaganda minister Joseph Goebbels during World War II, it was Winston Churchill who popularized it through his 'Sinews of Peace' address at a US college in 1946, although he had used it previously in private correspondence:

'An "iron curtain" has descended across the Continent. Behind that line lie all the capitals of the ancient states of Central and Eastern Europe. Warsaw, Berlin, Prague, Vienna, Budapest, Belgrade, Bucharest and Sofia; all these famous cities and the populations around them lie in what I must call the Soviet sphere, and all are subject, in one form or another, to Soviet influence.'

# BRITAIN AT WAR

---

## My kingdom for a horse

During World War I, over 8 million horses died. Trench warfare, machine guns and barbed wire finally put paid to fighting on horseback. In northern France, the British launched one of the last significant cavalry charges in March 1918 when only four horses returned out of 150.

---

## Douglas Bader

Douglas Bader epitomized the national spirit during World War II. A fighter pilot in the RAF, he took part in the Battle of Britain despite losing both legs in a pre-war accident. (The entry in his logbook of that day in 1931 reads: 'Crashed slow-rolling near ground. Bad show.') Captured by the Germans, the disabled hero made so many attempts to escape that he had to be locked up in Colditz castle. Bader's biography is called *Reach for the Sky* and a film, starring Kenneth More, was made in 1956. Bader's artificial legs can now be found in the RAF Museum at Stafford.

### THE ANIMAL VC

The PDSA Dickin Medal was awarded 54 times from 1943 to 1949. The recipients were 32 pigeons, 18 dogs, three police horses and a cat called Simon, which 'served' aboard HMS *Amethyst* in 1949, 'disposing of many rats though wounded by shell blast'. Buster the spaniel was the last animal to win a 'VC', for finding a cache of arms in Iraq in 2003.

### SELECTED BRITISH CASUALTIES

NAPOLEONIC WARS *200,000* ◇ CRIMEAN WAR *22,182* ◇ BOER WAR *22,000* ◇ WORLD WAR I *730,000* ◇ WORLD WAR II *460,000* ◇ FALKLANDS WAR *248* ◇ GULF WAR *57*

---

### Wars of the Roses

Richard III was the last English king to die in combat, an event which came about during the Wars of the Roses, a series of civil wars fought between the House of Lancaster and the House of York over who should sit on the English throne that went on for 30 years between 1455 and 1485. The roses refer to the heraldic badges featuring the red rose of Lancaster and the white rose of York, but it's thanks to a Shakespeare play (*Henry VI Part I*) that the war is so named. Interestingly, during the war many fought under different heraldic banners, for example featuring red dragons and white boars rather than roses. It's difficult to say who won. While the York forces succeeded in putting Edward VI on the throne twice, it was only when Henry Tudor from the House of Lancaster became King Henry VII in 1485 and married Edward VI's daughter, Elizabeth of York, that things began to settle down. He reunited the royal houses and merged the rival symbols into a new emblem, the red and white rose of Tudor.

---

## CAVALIERS VS ROUNDHEADS: THE ENGLISH CIVIL WAR

In no other war has a bigger proportion of the British population been killed. Around 85,000 succumbed in battle, while another 100,000 died subsequently. And, for the first and only time in history, an English king was executed. Charles I was found guilty of high treason on January 30 1649 and beheaded in front of the Palace of Whitehall. Essentially, the war was fought out between Royalists known as Cavaliers under King Charles I and certain Parliamentarians known as Roundheads under Oliver Cromwell. Cromwell's side won the Battle of Worcester on 3 September 1651 and he was installed as a sort of pseudo-king, or Lord Protector. The monarchy was restored in 1660 after Cromwell's death and Charles II came to the throne, but it was thanks to the English Civil War that Parliament became central to how Britain is governed.

# LORD HORATIO NELSON

*'England expects that every man will do his duty.'*
Lord Horatio Nelson's message to his men before the Battle of Trafalgar

Born on September 29, 1758, Horatio Nelson first went to sea at the age of 12, became a captain at 20 and sailed as far afield as the West Indies and Canada in a naval career which culminated at the Battle of Trafalgar in 1805. Revered as one of Britain's greatest heroes, the sea-captain of the Napoleonic war is a true British icon, described by 19th century poet Alfred Tennyson as *'the greatest sailor since the world began'*. It's strange, therefore, that he suffered from seasickness all his life.

## The key battles Nelson won

| DATE | BATTLE | SHIP | TITLE |
| --- | --- | --- | --- |
| 14 February 1797 | Battle of St Vincent | HMS *Captain* | Commodore |
| 1 August 1798 | Battle of The Nile | HMS *Vanguard* | Rear Admiral |
| 2 April 1801 | Battle of Copenhagen | HMS *Elephant* | Vice Admiral |
| 21 October 1805 | Battle of Trafalgar | HMS *Victory* | Vice Admiral |

### THE EYE PATCH

Nelson never wore an eye patch. Nor was he entirely blind in one eye. And, contrary to what you might recall, the figure atop Nelson's column in Trafalgar Square bears no eye patch. Nelson damaged his right eye while fighting in Corsica in 1794, but could still see out of it and to all intents and purposes it looked 'normal'. The eye patch was an artistic flourish used to accentuate Nelson's war wounds and air of heroism in paintings. He did, however, lose his right arm at the Battle of Santa Cruz de Tenerife in 1797, where it was amputated without anaesthetic.

## THE BATTLE OF TRAFALGAR

On 21 October 1805 Britain won one of its most decisive naval battles ever at Trafalgar. Some 1,700 British sailors were killed or wounded, but no British ships were lost, whereas 18 ships from the French and Spanish fleets were captured.

---

### Nelson's numerical legacy

In cricket and darts the score 111 is often referred to as 'a Nelson' or 'Nelson's'. Multiples are called 'double Nelson', 'triple Nelson', etc. One theory is that the three ones refer to Nelson only having one eye, one arm and one ball, by the end of his life. The other is that it refers to three consecutive victories (Copenhagen, Nile and Trafalgar), which he 'won, won and won'.

---

## NELSON'S ADVENTURES AFTER DEATH

*Killed by a French sniper's bullet at Trafalgar, Nelson's body was preserved in a cask of brandy on the journey back. Although it was under armed guard, there were rumours that sailors sampled the alcoholic contents of the barrel through straws. This is where the naval slang* 'tapping the admiral'*, or sneaking a sly drink, comes from. He is buried in St Paul's Cathedral in a coffin made with planks from the French ship* L'Orient*, blown up at the Battle of the Nile in 1798.*

---

### England expects...

On the morning of the 21st October, Nelson ran up a 31-flag signal to his fleet to rouse his troops. He originally planned the message as 'Nelson confides that every man will do his duty', but decided 'Nelson' was too personal and 'confides' too tricky a signal to convey. Instead, the flags read: 'England expects that every man will do his duty.'

---

# A BRIEF HISTORY OF THE UNION JACK

At more than 400 years old the Union Jack is one of the world's oldest national flags and simply consists of three flags – England, Scotland and Northern Ireland – mixed together. Its original name was actually the Union Flag, as opposed to the Union Jack. The Welsh flag isn't represented because Wales was legally already part of England when the original Union Flag was designed in 1606 to represent the union between England and Scotland under a common king, King James. The 1606 version simply consisted of the red cross of England superimposed upon the blue cross of Scotland. It was hugely unpopular with both the English and the Scots, each resenting their flag being obscured by the other. It fell even further out of favour when Oliver Cromwell abolished it along with the monarchy in 1649. But when the king returned, so, too, did the Union Jack. The cross of St Patrick was only added in 1801, following the Act of Union with Ireland. Since then the blue has got darker and the size of the stripes has changed, but it's essentially remained the same emblem.

## Why is it called the Union Jack?

The flag most likely gained its nickname at sea as originally it was designed only to be flown by English and Scottish ships. It wasn't until the official Act of Union between England and Scotland in 1707 that it began to be flown on land. Before then, it was flown from the 'jack' staff at the bow end of a ship and national flags flown by warships are often known as 'jacks'. Others rubbish this story and say it's derived from the Latin *jacobus* meaning James after the king who had it created, while some insist it's associated with the military 'jack-et'. In any case, its name has never officially been recognized as the Union Jack, although in 1908 a statement in Parliament declared that 'the Union Jack should be regarded as the national flag', which was reinforced again in 1933.

## OTHER JACKS

The Union Jack is featured in various other flags:

NATIONAL FLAG OF AUSTRALIA ◇ NATIONAL FLAG OF NEW ZEALAND ◇ NATIONAL FLAG OF TUVALU ◇ NATIONAL FLAG OF FIJI ◇ FLAGS OF THE CANADIAN PROVINCES: BRITISH COLUMBIA, MANITOBA AND ONTARIO ◇ STATE FLAG OF HAWAII

### Union Jack boxer shorts and all that

The image of a sunburnt British tourist strutting down the beach in Union Jack boxer shorts emerged in the late 20th century, but these days it's not only boxers that bear the Union Jack design. You can buy all manner of Jack-patterned gear, including doormats, removable tattoos, sunglasses and inflatable guitars. In Japan and curiously in one pub in Ledbury, Herts you can also purchase Union Jack-emblazoned condoms. Strangely, although you can print a Union Jack on pretty much anything, it is illegal to fly one from a British boat, a leftover from a 17th-century law to stop civilian ships flying one to imitate naval vessels and avoid harbour duties.

---

SPECIFIC DATES ON WHICH THE UNION JACK SHOULD BE FLOWN

20 January *Birthday of the Countess of Wessex* ❖ 6 February *Anniversary of the accession of Queen Elizabeth II* ❖ 19 February *Birthday of the Duke of York* ❖ Second Sunday in March *Commonwealth Day* ❖ 2 March *St David's Day* ❖ 10 March *Birthday of Prince Edward, Earl of Wessex* ❖ 17 March *St Patrick's Day* ❖ 21 April *Birthday of Queen Elizabeth II* ❖ 23 April *St George's Day* ❖ 9 May *Europe Day* ❖ 2 June *Anniversary Queen Elizabeth II's coronation* ❖ 10 June *Birthday of Prince Philip, Duke of Edinburgh* ❖ 16 June *Official Birthday of Queen Elizabeth II* ❖ 17 July *Birthday of the Duchess of Cornwall* ❖ 15 August *Birthday of the Princess Royal* ❖ Second Sunday in November *Remembrance Sunday* ❖ 14 November *Birthday of the Prince of Wales* ❖ 20 November *Wedding anniversary of Queen Elizabeth II and Prince Philip* ❖ 30 November *St Andrew's Day*

Source: Department for Culture, Media and Sport

# GREATEST NATIONAL RIVALS

*'Hell is a place where the motorists are French, the policemen are German and the cooks are English.'* Anon

While there is a strong degree of rivalry, animosity and general ill-feeling between the countries that make up Britain, even fiercer feeling is elicited from certain rivals overseas.

## GERMANY

*'Two world wars and one World Cup.'* This mantra isn't just chanted by England football fans. It's sort of an informal history lesson ingrained into every Brit as they grow up. Of course it was the two world wars that served to encourage downright dislike between Germany and Britain, but high-profile football games have done nothing to douse the flames of rivalry. The 1966 World Cup final was the catalyst. An epic match in which England triumphed was mired in controversy, mainly thanks to a dubious Geoff Hurst goal that may or may not have crossed the goal line. Germany got their revenge in the next World Cup in 1970, knocking England out in the semi-final and then again in 1990 and at Euro 96. Germany also won the last-ever game at the old Wembley Stadium during World Cup

qualifying, although that blow was softened somewhat as England walloped Germany 5–1 in Munich in the reverse fixture. *'Don't mention the score,'* screamed the headline from the *News of the World*.

*'The reason French roads have trees planted down both sides is that the Germans like to march in the shade.'* Anon

## FRANCE

When the Channel Tunnel opened in 1994, it brought together two countries that hadn't been physically connected since the Ice Age. It also linked two nations that historically hate each other. Forget the fact that the English call the French *frogs* and insist they smell of garlic, while the French label the English ignorant *rosbifs*; it goes deeper than that. Don't forget the two countries have been at war for much of their existence. And, even during the hundred years of the *Entente Cordiale* (an alliance that saw the countries side together in two world wars) contempt has never been far from the surface. Sure, there's mutual respect, as Peter Ustinov said: *'The French and the British are such good enemies that they can't resist being friends.'* But, there's also an awful lot of mutual disdain, akin to two brothers that can't stand the sight of each other.

### Argentina

*'An Argentine is an Italian who speaks Spanish and thinks he is British,'* goes the Latin American saying. Try telling an Argentinian this. The animosity between Argentina and Britain is relatively recent. It started with the Falklands War in 1982, but probably would have subsided if England hadn't kept getting drawn against Argentina in the World Cup. The football rivalry actually started way earlier. England beat Argentina 1–0 on their way to winning the World Cup in 1966, but during the ill-tempered match the Argentinian captain was sent off and the England manager, Alf Ramsey, described his opponents as 'animals'. The next time the two sides met in the World Cup, four years after the Falklands, things looked even worse. 'We knew a lot of Argentinian kids had died there, shot down like little birds,' said Diego Maradona, before putting England out by punching the ball into the back of the net – the 'Hand of God' goal. The sides have met in the World Cup twice since then, each winning once, which has only served to further heighten the rivalry.

# THE BRITISH EMPIRE

By 1921, the British Empire included about one-quarter of the world's population – approximately 458 million people – and covered about a quarter of the earth's total land area (36.6 million km), according to Angus Maddison in his book *The World Economy: A Millennial Perspective.* Although nowadays all this has changed greatly, British influence can still be seen all over the world in terms of political and legal systems, the ubiquity of the English language and sport and culture. Much of it may have been built originally on bloodshed and war, but this is the legacy of the British Empire.

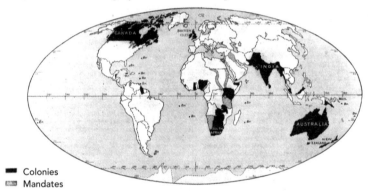

■ Colonies
▨ Mandates

*'The sun never sets on the British Empire.'*
This popular phrase stems from a comment made, not by a Brit, but by a half-Flemish Spaniard, Charles V, Holy Roman Emperor and King of Spain. In the 16th century he declared, *'In my realm the sun never sets,'* in reference to his far-reaching territories. It was during the Victorian era, when it was at its peak, that it became a popular phrase to describe the British Empire. The famous retort (which has been alternately accredited to the French or Sri Lankan lawyer Colvin R. de Silva) is: *'That's because God does not trust the British in the dark.'*

## Top 10 modern empires in terms of size

**British Empire** – 36 million sq km (under King George V in 1921)
**Russian Empire** – 22.8 million sq km (under Alexander III in 1895)
**Spanish Empire** – 19 million sq km (under Phillip II)
**Qing Empire** – 12 million sq km (under Emperor Qianlong)

**French Empire** – 12 million sq km
**Portuguese Empire** – 10.4 million sq km
**American Empire** – 10 million sq km (1898–1902 and 1906–1908)
**Japanese Empire** – 7.4 million sq km (during World War II)
**Mughal Empire** – 4 million sq km

## THE SCOTTISH EMPIRE

William Paterson was the ambitious man who founded the Bank of England. But when he concocted a plan to colonize the isthmus of Darien in what is now Panama he was out of his depth. The English didn't want to upset the Spanish in the area, so Paterson decided that Scotland alone would set up this trading hub and raised £400,000 to do so. In November 1698, 1,200 settlers arrived to find a humid, mosquito-infested swamp rife with tropical disease. You could barely breathe, let alone live or farm there. They called it New Caledonia. Within six months 200 settlers were dead and by the summer of 1699 the colony was abandoned. Just one of the five ships that had originally set sail returned with only 300 passengers. The rest of the would-be New Caledonians were dead and the Scottish economy was now about £250,000 in debt. As for Darien, it's still a savage, inhospitable place covered in jungle.

*'This door of the seas and the key of the universe will of course enable the proprietors to give laws to both oceans and to become arbitrators of the commercial world.'*
William Paterson on how his ill-fated scheme would transform Scotland

# BRITS ABROAD

*'Her Britannic Majesty's Secretary of State requests and requires in the Name of Her Majesty all those whom it may concern to allow the bearer to pass freely without let or hindrance and to afford the bearer such assistance and protection as may be necessary.'*

Inscription on a British passport

As great as many believe Britain is, her inhabitants have always been happy to travel abroad and settle overseas. Whether it's the high cost of living, the persistently poor weather or something else entirely, according to a number of sources more and more Brits are moving abroad.

In 2005 the Institute for Public Policy Research estimated that 5.5 million British people, equivalent to almost one in 10 of the population, were living abroad permanently. According to its research about 41 nations, including such unlikely candidates as Bulgaria, have at least 10,000 British residents. Here are the top eight:

| COUNTRY NAME | RESIDENT BRITONS |
|---|---|
| *Australia* | 1,300,000 |
| *Spain* | 761,000 |
| *United States* | 678,000 |
| *Canada* | 603,000 |
| *Ireland* | 291,000 |
| *New Zealand* | 215,000 |
| *South Africa* | 212,000 |
| *France* | 200,000 |

## NICKNAMES FOR THE BRITISH

♦ **LIMEY** *Used in US, Canada, Australia, New Zealand, South Africa*

As befits an island race, Brits have always made good sailors, hence the notion of Britannia ruling the waves. The nickname 'limey' was first bestowed on British sailors in the 19th century, a reference to the practice of issuing sailors with limes (cheaper than lemons at the time) to prevent scurvy, which was rife in the Royal Navy.

♦ **ROSBIF** *Used in France*

A reference to the legendary British fondness for roast beef.

♦ **ROOINEK** *Used in South Africa*

Afrikans for 'red neck'. This is a reference to the propensity of British settlers to suffer from sunburn in South Africa during the 19th century .

♦ **BIFE** *Used in Portugal*

Another reference to the legendary British fondness for roast beef. Female tourists are known as *bifas*.

♦ **ANGREZ** *Used in India*

Angrez is a word of Arabic or Persian origin to describe Brits, although it strictly means English.

Previously, *firangi* (alien) or *gora* (white person) were popular nicknames for Brits.

♦ **LOS GUIRIS** *Used in Spain*

Derogatory term for the Brit abroad.

♦ **LINKSRIJIERS** *Used in Holland*

A reference to the British habit of driving on the left.

♦ **FAJFOKLOK** *Used in Poland*

An obscure nickname, which may derive from the British obsession with punctuality.

♦ **POMMY** *Used in Australia, New Zealand*

'Pommy' or 'pom' is not altogether complimentary, and the etymology is unclear. One theory is that it is short for pomegranate, which is either loose rhyming slang for immigrant or a reference to the colour of the average Brit's skin after a day in the Australasian sun. Another theory is that it is an acronym for 'Prisoner Of Her Majesty'.

♦ **INSELAFFE** *Used in Germany*

Translates as 'island monkey'.

♦ **PIRATAS** *Used in Argentina*

This likens Brits to pirates, which stems from the Falklands War.

# SIR FRANCIS DRAKE

Probably born during the 1540s, Francis Drake lived an eventful life. He was a sailor and a slave trader, a pirate and a politician. In 1581 he was knighted by Queen Elizabeth I after becoming the first Englishman to circumnavigate the globe (and survive) and was then second-in-command of the English fleet when they beat the Spanish Armada in 1588. Legend has it that Drake was also the first Englishman to see the Pacific Ocean, climbing a high tree in the mountains in Panama to do so. Drake liked fighting and, even as he died of dysentery in 1596, he was still busy planning raids against Spanish ships off Puerto Rico.

> **Drake's legacy:** The Latin phrase on the coat of arms of Devon (where Drake was born) is *Auxilio Divino* meaning *'By Divine Aid'*, supposedly Drake's motto.

## DRAKE'S DARK SIDE

Although revered as a legendary Brit, Drake made his fortune in the 1550s along with his cousin Sir John Hawkins by trading West Africans as slaves. Then, in 1575, 600 Irish men, women and children were massacred by English troops on Rathlin Island after they had surrendered. Although the attack was led by Commander John Norreys, Drake was present and in charge of the ships transporting troops. Of course Drake probably committed a number of other atrocities. Pirates are not renowned for compassion and he was at war with Spain for most of his life. In Spanish, *El Draqui*, a bastardization of Drake, is a bogeyman used to scare children.

## The famous game of bowls

Legend has it that when the Spanish Armada was sighted off the coast of England Drake was busy playing a game of bowls on Plymouth Hoe and before going off to defeat the Spanish he finished his game. Whether or not this is true, British bravado and a game of bowls were not behind the delay. The English fleet didn't launch immediately since, due to a south-westerly wind and adverse tidal conditions, the ships were unable to leave the harbour.

## NOVA ALBION

BE IT KNOWN UNTO ALL MEN BY THESE PRESENTS JUNE 17 1579 BY THE GRACE OF GOD AND IN THE NAME OF HER MAJESTY QUEEN ELIZABETH OF ENGLAND AND HER SUCCESSORS FOREVER I TAKE POSSESSION OF THIS KINGDOM WHOSE KING AND PEOPLE FREELY RESIGN THEIR RIGHT AND TITLE IN THE WHOLE LAND AND UNTO HER MAJESTY'S KEEPING NOW NAMED BY ME AND TO BE KNOWN UNTO ALL MEN AS NOVA ALBION FRANCIS DRAKE

So reads a plaque found in the hills surrounding San Francisco in 1936. Allegedly, Drake left such a plaque in California, claiming the land for the queen as *Nova Albion* or 'New England'. The plaque was said to have had an English sixpence embedded in the right-hand corner, but now there is only a hole where the sixpence once was. Originally deemed authentic, scientists in the 1970s pronounced it a hoax.

## Will Drake return?

*In a variation on the sleeping hero myth, in English folklore it is said that if England is ever in grave danger that beating Drake's Drum will cause him to return to save the country.*

# EXPLORERS AND ADVENTURERS

From privateers such as Sir Francis Drake and gentleman explorers of the ilk of Dr David Livingstone to dashing modern-day professionals such as Ranulph Fiennes, there is a long line of notable British explorers and adventurers.

■ **Captain Tobias Furneaux** *(1735–1781)* An English navigator and naval officer, Furneaux was the first man to circumnavigate the world in both directions and also went on expeditions with Captain James Cook.

■ **Sir Alexander Mackenzie** *(1764–1820)* An explorer and fur trader, in 1793 Mackenzie led the first expedition to successfully make the trip north of Mexico across the North American continent from the Atlantic into the Pacific.

■ **John Fearn** *(1768–1837)* British naval officer Fearn 'discovered' the Pacific island of Nauru in 1798, which he named Pleasant Island due to its picturesque setting and the amiability of its inhabitants.

■ **Edward Bransfield** *(1785–1852)* A master in the Royal Navy. While sailing in the very south of the southern hemisphere in 1820, Bransfield made a note in his log of two *'high mountains, covered with snow'*. He had discovered Antarctica.

■ **Robert Falcon Scott** *(1868–1912)* Known as *'Scott of the Antarctic'*, the scientist and explorer came second behind the Norwegian Roald Amundsen in their race to reach the South Pole in 1912. More tragically he and all his party perished while attempting to return to their base. In Scott's journal, which was retrieved after his death he wrote: *'Had we lived I should have had a tale to tell of the hardihood, endurance and courage of my companions which would have stirred the heart of every Englishman.'*

■ **Colonel Noel Andrew Croft** *(1906–1998)* The inspiration for James Bond, Croft held the record for the longest, self-sustaining journey across the Arctic for more than 60 years. In 1953 he stood down from the Everest Expedition that Sir Edmund Percival Hillary went on and thus missed out on the chance of becoming one of the first men to climb Everest.

■ **Sebastian Snow** *(1929–2001)* Snow was excused from National Service at the age of 22 due to a sports injury, but this seemed to have had little effect on him when he became the first person to travel the length of the Amazon River.

■ **Lucy Walker** *(1836–1916)* Walker began climbing in 1858 at the age of 22 when her doctor suggested walking might help her rheumatism. She took his advice to heart and in 1871 became the first woman to conquer the Matterhorn.

■ **Lady Houston** *(1857–1936)* Born Fanny Lucy Randall, Lady Houston was an ex-showgirl and millionaire who funded the first aeroplane flight over the summit of Everest in 1933. An active suffragette as well as an enthusiastic supporter of Mussolini, she was declared mentally unfit to manage her own affairs after Sir Robert Houston died in 1926, leaving her an inheritance of approximately £5.5 million.

■ **Joseph Thomson** *(1858–1895)* '*He who goes gently, goes safely; he who goes safely goes far.*' This was the motto of Thomson, a Scottish geologist who explored much of Africa and has an African gazelle, '*Thomson's Gazelle*', named after him.

■ **Sir Francis Chichester** *(1901–1972)* On 28 May 1967 at the grand old age of 66, Chichester became the first person to circumnavigate the world solo. He had been diagnosed with terminal lung cancer in 1958 and died five years after setting the record.

■ **Sir Ranulph Fiennes** *(born 1944)* The holder of various endurance records and a distant cousin of the royal family, Fiennes is a farmer, author and explorer and the first man to visit the North and South Poles by land, covering 52,000 miles using only surface transport. A former SAS soldier he admits to cheating on the SAS endurance test known as 'Long Drag'. He is not averse to pain, however. Following

a failed expedition to the North Pole in 2000, Fiennes amputated some of his own frostbitten fingers with a fretsaw. Three years later, at the age of 59, he ran seven marathons in seven days across seven continents and then, in 2005, he ascended 28,500 feet in an attempt to conquer Everest.

■ **David Hempleman-Adams** *(born 1956)* Hempleman-Adams is the first man ever to reach the geographic and magnetic North and South Poles and to fly a hot air balloon over the North Pole. He's also climbed the seven highest peaks in each of the seven continents, made several Arctic expeditions and flown across the Atlantic Ocean in a hot air balloon. But perhaps his strangest feat is to have staged the world's highest formal dinner party. In June 2005 Hempleman-Adams, along with fellow explorer Bear Grylls and Lieutenant Commander Alan Veal rose to 24,000 feet in a hot air balloon dressed in formal attire. They then climbed out of the balloon, down to a dinner table suspended 40 feet below and dined on asparagus, duck and summer fruits.

■ **Ffyona Campbell** *(born 1967)* It took more than 11 years, but on the 14 October 1994 Campbell became the first woman to walk around the world, covering more than 20,000 miles. Except she didn't. Not exactly. It turned out that, on the US leg, she fell pregnant and it affected her walking so that between New York and LA she took secret lifts from a support vehicle to meet sponsor commitments. In 1996 she admitted cheating and returned to the US to re-walk the leg.

■ **Bear Grylls** *(born 1974)* Before Jake Meyer beat his record, former SAS soldier Grylls was the youngest-ever Brit to climb Everest.

■ **Jake Meyer** *(born 1984)* At the age of 21 years and four months, Meyer became the youngest Briton to climb Everest and the youngest-ever male to climb the seven highest mountains in each of the seven continents.

■ **Michael Perham** *(born 1992)* On 3 January 2007, at the age of 14, Michael Perham became the youngest person to single-handedly sail across the Atlantic. His trip started from Gibraltar, ended in Antigua and took six-and-a-half weeks.

### 'Dr Livingstone, I presume?'

Many gentlemen in the 19th century pursued a number of interests and David Livingstone was no exception. He was a missionary, a doctor, an explorer, a scientist and an anti-slavery activist. Born in Scotland in 1813, he spent 30 years of his life in Africa and was supposedly the first white man to see Victoria Falls: he gave it that name after Queen Victoria. One of his ambitions, which he never fulfilled, was to see the source of the Nile. It was while engaged on this task that the *New York Herald Tribune* sent Henry Stanley on a mission to locate Livingstone. It took two years, but in 1871 Stanley found him in Tanzania and supposedly uttered the legendary refrain, 'Dr. Livingstone, I presume?' Despite Stanley's attempts to persuade him to return home, Livingstone refused and, riddled with malaria and internal bleeding, died two years later.

## THE MAD YORKSHIREMAN

Born in Bradford, Maurice Wilson served in World War I, then moved to New Zealand to run a women's clothes shop, before deciding his destiny was to conquer Everest. In the 1930s he announced that he planned to crash-land a plane on its slopes before walking to the summit and planting a silken Union Jack there. This plan had fundamental problems: he'd never flown a plane before or completed any serious climbing. Displaying indomitable British spirit, however, he flew to India in a Gypsy Moth named *Ever-Wrest*. Financial constraints forced him to sell the plane, so he decided to rely on faith. Setting up camp on Everest, he maintained fasting and prayer would get him to the top. They didn't. He was found dead on the slopes the following year. There are rumours Wilson's body was found in women's underwear with other items of women's wear in his baggage. Then, in 1960 a woman's shoe was found at 21,000 feet, fuelling speculation that when Wilson set out to climb Everest he did so as a woman.

# CHARLES DARWIN

Born in Shrewsbury in 1809, Charles Darwin is best known for his pioneering work on the theory of evolution. But the only reason that he was able to form and develop his theories about natural selection was because he followed in a distinguished line of British explorers and travelled the world. Leaving Britain at 22, Darwin spent four years, nine months and five days as a resident naturalist aboard the HMS *Beagle* from 1831 to 1836, visiting South America, Australia, New Zealand, Tahiti and South Africa. This trip proved the inspiration for his achievements.

*'As far as I can judge of myself I worked to the utmost during the voyage from the mere pleasure of investigation, and from my strong desire to add a few facts to the great mass of facts in natural science.'*
Charles Darwin writing about the voyage of the *Beagle*

---

### DARWIN'S PALL-BEARERS

When Darwin was buried at Westminster Abbey in the same cemetery as John Herschel and Sir Isaac Newton, the pall-bearers included the Duke of Argyll, the American ambassador to Britain, James Lowell, Joseph Hooker, Thomas Huxley, Sir John Lubbock, Lord Derby and the Duke of Devonshire.

---

### Harriet the tortoise

In 1835 Charles Darwin captured three tortoises on the Galapagos Islands and took them to Britain. One of these, Harriet, wound her way back to the southern hemisphere and Australia with the retired captain of the *Beagle*, John Wickham, and first lived in the Botanic Gardens in Brisbane and then at the late Steve Irwin's zoo in Queensland. She died in June 2006, the oldest living animal in captivity with an estimated age of 175 years.

## Tastes like chicken

Owl, armadillo, puma, ostrich and tortoise are just a few of the animals Darwin tucked into. He got a taste for exotic meat while at Cambridge University as a member of the Glutton Club, which sought to sample animal flesh not normally found on a menu. Once he left Britain, he was given ample opportunity to extend his experimental eating. Armadillo, according to Darwin tasted like duck, while puma he likened to veal. On Darwin's birthday, 12 February, many Darwin disciples enjoy a 'Phylum Feast', a meal involving as many different species as possible.

## DARWIN'S LEGACY

Some things named after Darwin:

♦ **Darwin Sound:** *Expanse of seawater near Chile, linking the Beagle Channel to the Pacific Ocean.*

♦ **Mount Darwin:** *Highest peak in Tierra del Fuego, Chile.*

♦ **Port Darwin:** *Natural harbour in Australia, so named by Captain John Wickham of the HMS Beagle.*

♦ **Darwin:** *Capital city of Australia's Northern Territory, officially renamed Darwin instead of Palmerston in 1911. Now, it also boasts Charles Darwin University and Charles Darwin National Park.*

♦ **Darwin's Finches:** *14 closely related species of finch which Darwin first collected in the Galapagos Islands.*

♦ **Darwin College:** *The Cambridge college was founded in 1964.*

♦ **£10 note:** *In 2000, Darwin's image replaced that of Charles Dickens. Apparently the beard is tricky to forge.*

♦ **Darwin Award:** *A humorous accolade awarded annually to individuals that 'improve our gene pool by removing themselves from it'.*

♦ **Darwin's Frog:** *Frog native to Chile and Argentina, which raises tadpoles inside the vocal sac of the male.*

 Darwin did his bit for the propagation of his own species, fathering 10 children, two of whom died in childbirth.

# PETS, BIG CATS AND THE LOCH NESS MONSTER

## It's raining fish and frogs

Fish downpours are thought to be caused by a rare weather phenomenon whereby a small tornado, known as a waterspout, scoops up aquatic life before depositing the cargo as it moves above dry land and loses its energy. Here are just a few reports of strange showers in Britain:

❖ *'I was startled by something falling all over me – down my neck, on my head, and on my back. On putting my hand down my neck I was surprised to find they were little fish. By this time I saw the whole ground covered with them. We did gather a great many, about a bucketful, and threw them into the rain pool, where some of them now are.'*
EYEWITNESS ACCOUNT OF A FISH SHOWER IN GLAMORGAN IN WALES IN 1859

❖ Jellyfish fell from the sky in Bath in 1894.

❖ In 1984, flounders, lifted from the Thames, rained on London.

❖ In Norfolk during August 2000 a storm of two-inch sprats poured down upon the seaside town of Great Yarmouth.

❖ In August 2004, a deluge of fish fell on the town of Knighton, which straddles the English–Welsh border.

❖ *'Mr E. Ettles, superintendent of the municipal swimming pool, stated that he was caught in a heavy shower of rain and, while hurrying to shelter, heard a sound as of the falling of lumps of mud. Turning, he was amazed to see hundreds of tiny frogs falling on to the concrete path around the bath. Later, many more were found to have fallen on the grass nearby.'*
TROWBRIDGE, 16 JUNE 1939 AS REPORTED IN *THE METEOROLOGICAL MAGAZINE*

 In 2004 it was estimated that there were 20,000 wild parrots living in Britain that had been released by their owners.

## BIRDWATCHING

Birdwatching is a hugely popular pastime in Britain with its own clubs, competitions and code. The Royal Society for the Protection of Birds claims to have more than one million members, while Britain has 176 bird clubs and something like 20,000 people who watch birds, ranging from the diehard birder to those who are satisfied with just monitoring the birds in their garden.

## BIRD TALK

*'Twitching'* is the term used to describe the pursuit of a rare bird. While a rare bird is watchable it is called *'twitchable'*. A *'dip out'* or being *'dipped'* is how twitchers describe missing a rare bird. A twitcher is *'gripped off'* if he/she misses a rare bird, while fellow twitchers see it. A twitcher who neglects to inform other twitchers about news concerning a rare bird is indulging in *'suppression'*, while a *'dude'* is someone who is ignorant about rare birds or on their first twitching outing.

### Some famous birdwatchers

• The British spy **Harry St. John Bridger Philby**, also known as **Jack Philby** or **Sheikh Abdullah** • The former Prime Minister, **Harold Wilson** • **Ian Fleming**, who named his infamous character after the ornithologist James Bond • The English singer/songwriter **Billy Fury** • The comedian **Eric Morecambe**, whose statue is wearing binoculars on Morecambe seafront • The Conservative MP **Kenneth Clarke**

 One in three British pets are overweight and 82 per cent of vets run special clinics for overweight pets, according to a survey carried out in 1996.

## The Loch Ness Monster

Although internationally famous, there's no actual proof the Loch Ness Monster exists. First photographed in 1933 (which was later proved a hoax) rumours of a huge sea serpent in Loch Ness had been around for decades and, maybe, centuries. Despite many claimed sightings and scientific studies, there is no hard evidence that a sea monster lives in a lake near Inverness. This hasn't stopped a cult developing around 'Nessie', however, with an Official Loch Ness Monster Fan Club, diehard Nessie-watchers and various theories about what lives in the loch. One of the most popular is that it's related to the water-based dinosaur, the plesiosaur, while others suggest it's an overgrown eel. And, while no one has ever proved its existence, there is no proof to the contrary either.

## PETS

Britain is a nation of pet-owners, famed for its love of animals. Whereas other nations are infamous for their cruelty to animals, Brits are known for the devotion they demonstrate towards their pets. In particular Brits love dogs. While other countries boast forms of animal entertainment such as bullfights, dancing bears and monkeys dressed up as children, Britain has Crufts, the biggest and most famous dog show in the world where there is little cruelty, unless it's possible to groom an Old English Sheepdog to death on the morning of the competition. Here are the top 10 dog breeds in Britain, according to the Kennel Club:

1. Retriever *(Labrador)*
2. Spaniel *(Cocker)*
3. Spaniel *(English Springer)*
4. German Shepherd Dog *(Alsatian)*
5. Staffordshire Bull Terrier
6. Cavalier King Charles Spaniel
7. Retriever *(Golden)*
8. West Highland White Terrier
9. Boxer
10. Border Terrier

Rabbits are the most abused domestic pet in Britain with 35,000 pet rabbits abandoned every year, according to the RSPCA.

## BRITAIN'S BIG CATS

For years and years there have been reports of big cats  roaming around the British countryside. The last truly indigenous big cat, the leopard, became extinct in Britain more than 12,000 years ago, so many people quite understandably view such sightings as hoaxes or simply as an urban myth. Others believe they aren't animals at all, but ghosts. The introduction of the 1976 dangerous animals act, which made it more difficult to keep big cats as pets, however, could have led to owners setting them loose in the British countryside. And, exotic cats do escape from captivity from time to time, with the British Big Cats Society claiming there were 2,052 unconfirmed big cat sightings between January 2003 and March 2004.

---

### Dark Dartmoor

Dartmoor is a spooky place, haunted by pixies, phantom hounds, a headless horseman and a large black dog. Never mind the weather, add to that the hairy hands, which allegedly attack motorists on the B3212 near Two Bridges, and a reported visit by the Devil during the Great Thunderstorm of 1638 and you can see why people get scared of spending the night on the Moors. Arguably far more dangerous is the military activity, however, which dates back to the Napoleonic Wars. Parts of Dartmoor (not, thankfully, the national park) are used as a military firing range and have been for over 200 years.

---

# RIVERS AND NATIONAL PARKS

---

### The 10 longest rivers in Britain
**1.** River Severn 220/219 miles **2.** River Thames 215 miles **3.** River Trent 185 miles **4.** River Great Ouse 143 miles **5.** River Wye 135 miles **6.** River Tay 117 miles **7.** River Spey 107 miles **8.** River Clyde 106 miles **9.** River Tweed 96 miles **10.** River Nene 91 miles

---

## RIVER SEVERN

At 220 miles, the River Severn is Britain's longest river, pipping the River Thames by just five miles. Many believe its name is derived from Sabrina, the name of a nymph who drowned in the river in a mythical tale. As well as being its longest, the River Severn is also Britain's most dangerous river, with records suggesting it has claimed around 300 lives.

## THE THAMES

Thanks to cleaning initiatives, the River Thames is now home once again to 80 species of fish. It was the Victorians that turned the river bad, culminating in the Great Stink in the summer of 1858 when the river overflowed with raw sewage and the smell overwhelmed London. Between the 14th century and the 19th century, the River Thames froze over many times and festivals known as frost fairs were held on the ice. Henry VIII is supposed to have travelled all the way from central London to Greenwich by sleigh along the river in 1536, while Elizabeth I allegedly took walks on the ice in 1564.

---

 **On average, one dead body is found in the Thames every week.**

## The Peak District national park

Named as Britain's first ever national park in 1951, the Peak District is one of the country's most beautiful spots. It was the backdrop for a demonstration by radical ramblers back in 1932. They climbed Kinder Scout to demand public access to open spaces. Four of the militant hikers were arrested, but the law was changed thanks to the demo.

♦ **Dartmoor** (national park since 1951) *The largest area of open country in southern England, covering 368 square miles of land.*

♦ **Lake District** (national park since 1951) *All the land in England more than 3,000 feet above sea level lies in this national park in Cumbria.*

♦ **Snowdonia** (national park since 1951) *Home to Mount Snowdon.*

♦ **Pembrokeshire Coast** (national park since 1952)

♦ **Exmoor** (national park since 1954) *The Beast of Exmoor is reputed to haunt the moor, blamed for various acts of sheep slaying since the 1960s.*

♦ **Yorkshire Dales** (national park since 1954)

♦ **North York Moors** (national park since 1952)

♦ **Northumberland** (national park since 1956)

♦ **Brecon Beacons** (national park since 1957)

♦ **The Broads** (national park since 1988)

♦ **New Forest** (national park since 2005) *Has its own wild ponies.*

♦ **Scotland** *National parks were established in Loch Lomond and the Trossachs in 2002 and in the Cairngorms in 2003.*

## 10 English theme parks

American Adventure World, *Derbyshire* ★ Alton Towers, *Staffordshire* ★ Brocklands Adventure Park, *Bude* ★ Cadbury World, *Birmingham* ★ Camelot, *Lancashire* ★ Chessington World of Adventure, *Surrey* ★ Gullivers Theme Park, *Milton Keynes* ★ Legoland, *Windsor* ★ Oakwood, *Pembrokeshire* ★ Thorpe Park, *London* ★

# WHO WAS THE REAL ROBIN HOOD?

A Yorkshireman called Robert Hood, a knight named Robert Fitz Odo, an outlaw called Robert of Wetherby, a 13th-century fugitive nicknamed Hobbehod, a Shropshire Baron called Fulk fitz Warin and the Earl of Huntingdon can all lay claim to being the original figure behind the legend of Robin Hood. But none of their claims is entirely convincing. Passed down and embellished over the centuries through appearances in ballads, plays, books and films, the legend has taken on a life of its own and it's difficult to separate the man from the myth. Some believe that Robin Hood was merely a nickname for criminals or more than one outlaw used it as an alias, others that the Robin Hood story is simply an amalgamation of the exploits of real and imaginary outlaws. Although subjected to various treatments, the common story involves a bold outlaw who lives in Sherwood Forest along with his band of merry men and his wife, Maid Marian, constantly waging battle against his nemesis, the Sheriff of Nottingham. And, of course, as a champion of injustice he steals from the rich to give to the poor.

### Did Robin Hood wear green or red?

Although these days Robin Hood is traditionally associated with the colour green in *'A Gest or Robyn'* and other 15th century ballads, Robin Hood and his 'merry men' wore red. He only began to wear green in later versions of the tale.

## ROBIN HOOD'S GRAVE

In the grounds of Kirklees Priory lies an old gravestone of a *'Robard Hude'*, which some like to believe marks the final resting place of the 'real' Robin Hood. However, the tombstone is unlikely to date from the 13th century and the style and language suggest it is a poor 17th-century forgery.

## THE MAJOR OAK

In the centre of Sherwood Forest stands the Major Oak, a tourist attraction promoted as Robin Hood's hideout or headquarters. Although it weighs in at around 23 tons with a girth of 10 metres and a spread of 28 metres, which makes it the biggest oak tree in Britain, it is still too young to have been a 13th-century outlaw's home.

## OVERSEAS ANSWERS TO ROBIN HOOD

They may not shoot bow and arrows, have merry men or even a Maid Marian equivalent, but many countries have their own answer to Robin Hood:

ARGENTINA – *Che Guevara* ✳ AUSTRALIA – *Ned Kelly* ✳ RUSSIA – *Basil the Blessed* ✳ MEXICO – *Joaquin Murrieta* ✳ KOREA – *Hong Gil-dong* ✳ JAPAN – *Nezumi Kozo* ✳ ESTONIA – *Jüri Rummo* ✳ BOLIVIA – *Roberto Suarez Gomez*

## SHERWOOD FOREST VS BARNSDALE FOREST

Most people associate Robin Hood with Sherwood Forest, but some claim that it was in Barnsdale Forest in Yorkshire that Robin Hood had his hideout and made his home. This is because it is referenced in some of the early ballads that outline the legend of Robin Hood. While Sherwood Forest with its proximity to the Sheriff of Nottingham remains the favourite with tourists, South Yorkshire's airport is called the Robin Hood Airport.

 **The University of Nottingham offers a Masters degree on the subject of Robin Hood.**

# BRITISH INVENTIONS

## Some famous British inventors and their inventions

**1600s** William Gascoigne MICROMETER

**1764** James Hargreaves SPINNING JENNY

**1785** Joseph Bramah BEER PUMP

**1785** William Symington STEAMBOAT

**1790** Thomas Saint SEWING MACHINE

**1790** William Wouldhave/Lionel Lukin LIFEBOAT

**1802** Richard Trevithick STEAM LOCOMOTIVE

**1810** Peter Durand TIN CAN

**1813** Arthur Wynne CROSSWORD PUZZLE

**1821** Charles Macintosh WATERPROOF FABRIC

**1823** Samuel Brown INTERNAL COMBUSTION ENGINE

**1828** Thomas Fowler CENTRAL HEATING

**1830** Edward Beard Budding LAWN MOWER

**1837** Sir Isaac Pitman SHORTHAND

**1838** James Chalmers ADHESIVE POSTAGE STAMP

**1838** James Marsh TEST FOR DETECTING ARSENIC

**1843** Alexander Bain FAX MACHINE

**1845** Stephen Perry RUBBER BAND

**1860** Sir Joseph Swan LIGHT BULB

**1865** Robert William Thomson PNEUMATIC TYRE

**1871** John Tyndall GAS MASK

**1880** John Milne SEISMOGRAPH

**1885** John Kemp Starley MODERN BICYCLE

**1892** Sir James Dewar THERMOS FLASK

**1894** William Kennedy Dickson MOTION PICTURE CAMERA

**1901** Hubert Cecil Booth VACUUM CLEANER

**1901** E Purnell Hooley TARMAC

**1907** William Willett DAYLIGHT SAVING TIME

**1917** Harry Ferguson MODERN TRACTOR

**1928** Sir Alexander Fleming PENICILLIN

**1934** Percy Shaw CAT'S EYES

**1935** Robert Watson-Watt RADAR

**1953** Sir Christopher Cockerell HOVERCRAFT

**1967** John Shepherd-Barron ATM

**1990** Tim Berners-Lee WORLD WIDE WEB

## The guillotine

Although the guillotine is associated with the French Revolution, an almost identical device was invented in Britain long before the French started lopping off their royals' heads. In Halifax to be precise. Called the Halifax Gibbet, it featured an iron axe on a cross beam attached to a rope and pulley. Between 1541 and 1650 records suggest that 53 people were executed by the Gibbet. A similar device, known as the Scottish Maiden, was used to execute miscreants north of the border during the 16th and 17th centuries, while the guillotine didn't appear in France until the late 18th century.

## CHARLES BABBAGE (1791–1871)

Known as the father of computing, Charles Babbage invented the *'Difference Engine'*, a machine that was like a giant calculator, and designed the *'Analytical Engine'*, which comprised a memory unit and was intended to be able to perform any mathematical operation. His work laid the foundations for today's computers. A philosopher and code-breaker, Babbage was good friends with Charles Dickens and also something of a traditional British eccentric who once baked himself in an oven at 265F for *'five or six minutes without any great discomfort'*, to see what would happen. He hated street musicians with a passion including them in an essay entitled *'Observations of Street Nuisances'*. Other strange publications included a *Table of the Relative Frequency of the Causes of Breakage of Plate Glass Windows*, published in 1857.

 The inventor of the World Wide Web, Timothy Berners-Lee, played tiddlywinks for Oxford against Cambridge while at university. He was also banned from using the university computer after he was caught hacking.

## Dolly the Sheep

When a sheep was born in Scotland on 5 July 1995, she made history as the first-ever mammal to be successfully cloned. Using a technique called somatic cell nuclear transfer, scientists at the Roslin Institute in Midlothian, Scotland cloned *'Dolly'*, as she was called, from an old Finnish Dorset ewe. As it was a mammary cell she was cloned from, the sheep was named in honour of Dolly Parton. The cloned sheep died six years later and her stuffed remains reside in Edinburgh's Royal Museum.

## THE MAD SCIENTIST

Britain has produced its fair share of mad scientists and Geoffrey Pyke is a perfect example. Torpedo-transporting sledges and aircraft-carriers made from wood pulp and ice were just a couple of his unorthodox ideas for World War II. Winston Churchill was open-minded about his plan to construct unsinkable ships with hulls made of wood fibres and crystalline ice, but in the end they came to nothing. During the war, he suggested sending in a team of dogs disguised as wolves to scare away the soldiers guarding oil fields in Romania. If this didn't work, he recommended sending in a team of women to seduce them. Pyke was an incessant worker and often wouldn't waste time getting out of bed, instead inviting military personnel to his home for bedside conferences. Unfortunately, few of his ideas or inventions ever came to fruition and sadly, in 1948 at the age of 54, he shaved off his beard, swallowed a bottle of sleeping pills and bade farewell to a world that did not understand him.

 The first person to be killed in a parachuting accident was 61-year-old Brit, Robert Cocking, who died in 1837 testing out a parachute design he'd concocted.

The man who invented the first portable machine gun, Sir Hiram Stevens Maxim, also invented the humble mousetrap.

## The crossword puzzle

Although the first crossword puzzle appeared in an American newspaper called the *New York World* on 21 December 1913, it was invented by a Brit from Liverpool. Journalist Arthur Wynne emigrated to the USA and devised the first crossword puzzle on the other side of the Atlantic. He called his diamond-shaped invention the 'word-cross'.

## WHY DO SO MANY INVENTORS COME FROM SCOTLAND?

Forget about Irn-Bru and haggis, Scotland has given birth to some truly influential inventions. John Logie Baird, born in Argyll, was instrumental in the invention of television, as was Edinburgh-born Alexander Graham Bell in the development of the telephone. We have another Scot, Alexander Bain, to thank for the electric clock and the first fax machine. Considering the amount of rain that falls in Scotland, it's less surprising that one of its sons, Charles Macintosh, invented the waterproof bearing his name. Another practical invention, the adhesive postage stamp, was dreamt up by a Scotsman, James Chalmers. More recently, John Shepherd-Barron, devised the ATM.

## Penny Farthing

The Penny Farthing may not be the world's first bicycle, but it is a thoroughly British invention. Unveiled in 1871 by engineer James Starley, it was a particularly efficient contraption in comparison to other bicycles of the time, consisting of a large front wheel, which pivoted on a tubular frame, teamed with a small rear wheel. It also looked thoroughly ridiculous.

## 'Death Ray' Matthews

In 1924, an electronic engineer from Gloucestershire called Harry Grindell Matthews claimed to have invented a death ray which could shoot down aeroplanes, stop ships and decapitate soldiers from a distance of up to four miles. The problem was that Matthews wasn't keen on proving it worked. The British government was interested but sceptical, and Matthews refused to allow his alleged invention to undergo official testing. Instead, he threatened to sell it to the French, before decamping to the US. Again, no demonstrations materialized and, though Matthews claimed to have lost his left eye through experiments with the death ray, American scientists were not convinced and one professor offered to stand in front of the death ray device, arguing it simply didn't work. When Matthews returned to England in 1930, he claimed to have sold the death ray in the US, but wouldn't say to who, or for how much. This time he was armed with a gentler invention: the Sky Projector. This reportedly did work and he supposedly projected images of angels plus a Christmas message and a picture of a moving clock on to the sky above Hampstead. Ultimately, no one was interested in buying this either, however.

## THE VIAGRA CONTROVERSY

The American pharmaceutical company, Pfizer, may disagree, but many believe British scientists invented Viagra. It's certainly the names of two British scientists – Peter Dunn and Albert Wood – which appear on the patent application, but Pfizer claims hundreds were involved in creating Viagra and there was no room on the patent application to list them all. Another Brit, Dr Nicholas Terrett, is named on the 1991 British patent for a heart medicine, Sildenafil, later trade-named Viagra. The scientists refuse to comment on the specifics as they are still employed by Pfizer. More than US$1 billion was made in sales during Viagra's first year of production.

# THE BRITISH PUB

British culture may be difficult for outsiders to comprehend, but in order to understand it, you need to appreciate the central importance of the pub. There is no more popular pastime in Britain than visiting the pub. Brits have been drinking beer of sorts since the Bronze Age, but the first pubs functioning as inns for weary travellers arrived with the Romans. Britain has never looked back. Nowadays, Britain boasts more than 61,000 pubs frequented by more than three-quarters of the adult population. More than a third of those are regulars, who visit the pub at least once a week. In villages and towns all over Britain, pubs are at the centre of communities. The bar counter in the pub is one of the few places in Britain where friendly conversation with total strangers is considered socially appropriate and acceptable.

*'There is nothing which has yet been contrived by man, by which so much happiness is produced as by a good tavern or inn.'*
Samuel Johnson

## Pub signs

No British pub is complete without a sign, traditionally sporting a picture that illustrates the pub's name. The trend started in 1393 when King Richard II issued legislation that stated: 'Whosoever shall brew ale in the town with intention of selling it must hang out a sign, otherwise he shall forfeit his ale.' Much of the population was illiterate during the Middle Ages, so pictures were more useful than a written sign.

*'When you have lost your inns, drown your empty selves, for you will have lost the last of England!'*
Anglo-French writer Hilaire Belloc

# THE OLDEST PUB IN BRITAIN

A former pigeon coop that hosted cockfights and once boasted Oliver Cromwell as a guest. There are a number of pubs that claim to be the oldest pub in Britain, but 'Ye Olde Fighting Cocks Inn' in St Alban's, Hertfordshire is probably the most likely candidate and is listed as such in the *Guinness Book of Records*. Its foundations date from AD793 and parts of the building go back to the 11th century, although it has only sat in its present location since 1485 and been rebuilt since then. Formerly known as the Round House, it changed its name in the 1800s when cockfighting was at a popular peak. The following pubs also claim to be Britain's oldest:

THE BINGLEY ARMS, *Leeds, England* ◇ THE CLACHAN INN, *Loch Lomond, Scotland* ◇ THE EAGLE AND CHILD, *Gloucestershire, England* ◇ THE MAN AND SCYTHE, *Lancashire, England* ◇ THE OLD FERRYBOAT INN, *Cambridgeshire, England* ◇ THE SKIRRID MOUNTAIN INN, *Abergavenny, Wales* ◇ YE OLDE TRIP TO JERUSALEM, *Nottingham, England*

## The smallest pub in Britain

The Nutshell in Bury St Edmunds, Suffolk claims to be the smallest pub in Britain at 5 metres by 2 metres. There is, however, room to swing a cat and the suspended dried-out body of a black cat that was found while building work was in progress allegedly used to hang from the ceiling. The building is also apparently home to four ghosts – a young, blond-haired boy who lives on the third floor, a long-haired Victorian gentleman who haunts the second floor and a monk and nun who hang out in the cellar.

### SLANG TERMS FOR THE PUB

boozer ❖ battle cruiser ❖ the local ❖ watering hole ❖ nuclear sub ❖ rub-a-dub-dub

## TOP 5 PUB NAMES IN BRITAIN

The Red Lion ❖ The Crown ❖ The Royal Oak ❖ The White Hart ❖ The King's Head  Source: CAMRA

## POPULAR FICTIONAL PUBS

Tabard Inn, *Canterbury Tales,* Chaucer ❖ The Rovers Return, *Coronation Street* ❖ Queen Vic, *EastEnders* ❖ The Bull, *The Archers* ❖ The Woolpack, *Emmerdale*

## SOME NOTABLE BRITISH PUBS

♦ The Dove in Hammersmith may not be the smallest pub in Britain, but it boasts the smallest bar and was a favourite with both Ernest Hemingway and Graham Green.

♦ The George in Southwark in London was frequented by both William Shakespeare and Charles Dickens.

♦ The Mardens Grotto in South Shields in the Northeast of England is built into the cliff face with caves functioning as the bar and kitchen. Supposedly haunted by a smuggler, a former landlord allegedly used to leave a tankard of ale out each evening after closing, which would vanish by the morning.

♦ The Baltasound Hotel on the Shetland Islands is the most northerly in Britain. The Top House in Cornwall is the most southerly.

♦ The Clachan Inn, Loch Lomond claims to be the oldest pub in Scotland and to have once had Rob Roy's sister as a landlady.

♦ The Eagle and Child in Oxford was frequented by 'The Inklings' during the 20th century, a group of erudite writers which included J.R.R. Tolkien and C.S. Lewis, who met every Tuesday morning in the back room.

♦ The Tan Hill Inn in the Pennine Valley in North Yorkshire is the highest pub in Britain at 536 m above sea level.

# BOOZE BRITAIN

Britain has a formidable relationship with alcohol. From modern-day binge drinking to mid-18th century gin mania and inebriated Anglo-Saxon invaders, Brits have always known how to drink to excess. Over 90 per cent of British adults drink. Britain is a nation that goes out and gets drunk; it doesn't go out to drink, it goes out to get drunk. And booze is big business. The value of the drinks market to the UK economy was estimated at about £30bn in 2004 and alcohol taxes raise £7bn a year.

### percentage of drinkers that drink to get drunk
Wales & South West **33%** Northern England **28%** South East **24%**
Midlands **19%** Scotland **18%** *Source: Institute of Alcohol Studies, 2005*

## BINGE DRINKING

Binge drinking basically means getting blind drunk in a single session. The British custom of buying rounds is believed to contribute to binge drinking as it encourages everyone in the round to drink at the same rate as the fastest drinker and drink more than they otherwise might. Of course downing competitions, the excessive use of alcohol as a social crutch on which to lean while talking to members of the opposite sex and the lack of anything else to do on a Friday night in provincial towns are other contributory factors. But binge drinking doesn't come cheap. A government report in 2003 suggested that binge drinking is costing the country an estimated £20 billion per year and all indications suggest it's on the rise.

### BINGE DRINKING AS PERCENTAGE OF TOTAL

| COUNTRY | MEN | WOMEN |
|---------|-----|-------|
| UK | 40 | 22 |
| Sweden | 33 | 18 |
| Finland | 29 | 17 |
| Germany | 14 | 7 |
| Italy | 13 | 11 |
| France | 9 | 5 |

*Source: Institute of Alcohol Studies, 2005*

*'Binge drinking is now usually used to refer to heavy drinking over an evening or similar time span – sometimes also referred to as heavy episodic drinking. Binge drinking is often associated with drinking with the intention of becoming intoxicated and, sometimes, with drinking in large groups.'*

The British Medical Association

## Real ale

Foreigners might shake their heads at the British fondness for *'warm beer'*, but Brits have had a taste for real ale that predates the current vogue for chilled continental lagers. In fact, Brits have been quaffing a fermented barley brew of sorts since Roman times. Beer-brewing became a business for monasteries during the Middle Ages and for a long time, when the purity of water was dubious at best, beer was a core element in the British diet. Many would argue that it still is, although nowadays Brits are more likely to chuck 10 pints of imported lager down their necks on a Saturday night than drink a pint of real ale before they embark on a day's labour. The popularity of lager and the potential it has for eliminating real ales from British pubs is something that the Campaign for Real Ale (CAMRA) has been addressing since the 1970s. CAMRA argues that dismissing real ale as 'warm beer' misses the point: British beer and ale should be served slightly warmer so drinkers can enjoy the flavour.

*'The most expensive bottle of wine was sold at an auction at Christies, London, UK, in December 1985. The buyer paid £105,000 for a bottle of 1787 Chateau Lafite claret that was engraved with the initials of Thomas Jefferson. Eleven months after the sale, the cork dried out, slipped into the bottle and spoiled the wine, making it the most expensive bottle of vinegar!'*

The Guinness Book of Records, 1999

**Queen Elizabeth I used to drink real ale at breakfast.**

---

## DRINKING QUOTES

*'Let us have wine and women, mirth and laughter. Sermons and soda water the day after.'*
Lord Byron

*'Claret is the liquor for boys; port for men; but he who aspires to be a hero must drink brandy.'*
Samuel Johnson

*'An alcoholic is someone you don't like who drinks as much as you do.'*
Dylan Thomas

*'Beer glasses are by far the most common weapon of assault in Britain.'*
Jonathan Shepherd, University of Wales College of Medicine

*'The first draught serveth for health, the second for pleasure, the third for shame, the fourth for madness.'*
Sir Walter Raleigh

*'Alcohol is the anaesthesia by which we endure the operation of life.'*
George Bernard Shaw

*'If the headache preceded the intoxication, alcoholism would be a virtue.'*
Samuel Butler

*'It only takes one drink to get me drunk, but I can't remember if it's the 13th or 14th.'*
George Burns

*'We are fighting three foes – Germany, Austria and drink – and drink is most deadly of all.'*
Lloyd George during World War I

*'No animal ever invented anything as bad as drunkenness – or so good as drink.'*
G K Chesterton

# WHO INVENTED CHAMPAGNE?

One theory suggests that it was the English, and not the French, who originally invented champagne. The English were guzzling sparkling wine as far back as the 16th century, adding sugar and molasses to aid fermentation and fizz and producing bottles and corks strong enough to contain it. At the end of the 17th century, sparkling wine emerged in France, though the Royal Society claims the original *méthode champenoise* was first written down in England in 1662. As for the blind Benedictine monk Dom Perignon, he simply improved the method, rather than invented it. Brut, or modern champagne, was perfected in France in 1876, but even then it was for export to England. The UK remains France's biggest customer for champagne, representing a third of the export market and consuming 34 million bottles in 2004. Brits consume twice as much champagne as Americans and 20 times more than the Spanish.

## Pimms

Invented in 1823 by James Pimm who owned an oyster bar in central London, the drink was flavoured with herbs and quinine and originally designed as a digestive tonic. Quickly, it was being quaffed by the fashionable among Victorian society's upper middle class and it has never looked back. Pimms is now a traditional English summer drink.

## Alcohol and death

The following shows the proportion of deaths from alcohol-related causes in the UK per 100,000 people in periods since World War II:

| 1950–65 | | 1966–80 | | 1981–95 | | 1995 | |
|---|---|---|---|---|---|---|---|
| MEN | WOMEN | MEN | WOMEN | MEN | WOMEN | MEN | WOMEN |
| 0.3 | 0.1 | 1.2 | 0.5 | 2.2 | 0.8 | 2.8 | 1.1 |

*Source: Institute of Alcohol Studies, 2005*

# PUT THE KETTLE ON!

Drinking tea is something Brits are good at. We drink more than 160 million cups of the stuff every day and are famed the world over for our penchant for tea. Tea may have been invented in Asia, but in Europe Brits were early adopters and, by the 18th century, tea had replaced ale and gin as Britain's most popular beverage.

*'[I'm] a hardened and shameless tea-drinker, who has for twenty years diluted his meals with only the infusion of this fascinating plant, whose kettle scarcely has time to cool, who with Tea amuses the evening, with Tea solaces the midnights, and with Tea welcomes the morning.'*

Samuel Johnson expresses the views of many a tea-loving Brit

---

### The invention of the tea bag

Sadly, it was not a Brit, but an American, Thomas Sullivan who invented the tea bag in 1908. Unsurprisingly, considering the USA's lukewarm attitude to tea, he had no idea what he was doing. Sullivan sent samples of his tea to customers in small silken bags. Instead of extracting the loose leaves, they assumed the entire bag should be put in the pot. When they complained that the silk bags were too fine, Sullivan developed gauze and then perforated paper bags.

---

## TEA SMUGGLING

Before the 19th century, the tax on tea was so high that it encouraged a thriving black market. No duty was paid on tea smuggled into Britain and sophisticated smuggling networks developed in response to popular demand. More tea was smuggled into Britain than was imported legally. In 1785, after demands from legitimate tea merchants, the government slashed the duty on tea and tea smuggling was wiped out overnight.

*'Tea is one of the mainstays of civilization in this country.'*
George Orwell, *Evening Standard*, January 1946

## GEORGE ORWELL'S 11 RULES FOR THE PERFECT CUP OF TEA

• Use tea from India or Ceylon (Sri Lanka), not China • Use a teapot, preferably ceramic • Warm the pot over direct heat • Tea should be strong – six spoons of leaves per litre • Let the leaves move around the pot – no bags or strainers • Take the pot to the boiling kettle • Stir or shake the pot • Drink out of a tall, mug-shaped teacup • Don't add creamy milk • Add milk to the tea, not vice versa • No sugar!

---

### How to make a perfect cup of tea according to the Royal Society of Chemistry

**Ingredients:** *Loose-leaf Assam tea; soft water; fresh, chilled milk; white sugar.* **Implements:** *Kettle; ceramic teapot; large ceramic mug; fine mesh tea strainer; teaspoon, microwave oven.*

❶ Draw fresh, soft water and place in kettle and boil. Boil just the required quantity to avoid wasting time, water and power.

❷ While waiting for the water to boil, place a ceramic teapot containing a quarter of a cup of water in a microwave oven on full power for one minute.

❸ Synchronize your actions so that you have drained the water from the microwaved pot at the same time that the kettle water boils.

❹ Place one rounded teaspoon of tea per cup into the pot.

❺ Take the pot to the kettle as it is boiling, pour on to the leaves and stir.

❻ Leave to brew for three minutes.

❼ The ideal receptacle is a ceramic mug or your personal mug.

❽ Pour milk into the cup FIRST, followed by the tea, aiming to achieve a rich and attractive colour.

❾ Add sugar to taste.

❿ Drink at between 60–65 degrees C to avoid vulgar slurping which results from trying to drink tea at too high a temperature.

# CURRIED BRITAIN

In Britain curry almost possesses the status of a national dish. Curry houses exist on almost every high street and several dishes that curry fans think of as Indian in origin were actually invented in Britain. While ethnic restaurants are a 20th century phenomenon, the popularity of curry in Britain is a colonial legacy, dating back to the 18th century. Indian food was available in Britain before the 20th century, but the explosion in Indian restaurants occurred in the latter half of the 20th century when there was an influx of immigrants from Asia. It was then that curry began to take hold of the British culinary psyche and the British tradition of going for a curry and ordering the hottest dish on the menu after necking numerous pints in a pub was born.

• The first curry recipe published in Britain was in 1747 in *The Art of Cookery made Plain and Easy* by Hannah Glasse.

• Probably the first time curry appeared on a British menu was at the Coffee House in Norris Street, Haymarket, London in 1773.

• The first curry house in Britain, or restaurant dedicated to Indian cuisine, was *Hindostanee Coffee House* at 34 George Street, Portman Square, London, which opened in 1809.

**In London alone, there are more Indian restaurants than in Mumbai or Delhi.**

Chicken Tikka Masala is so popular in Britain that it is available as a pizza topping and a crisp flavour.

## CHICKEN TIKKA MASALA

This dish may involve traditional Asian ingredients and elements, but it was invented in Britain by Bangladeshi chefs in the late 1960s or early 1970s. One theory is that a chef simply added a creamy tomato gravy to a dry chicken tikka dish after a customer sent it back to the kitchen. Another is that it became a way for curry houses to recycle chicken tikka kebabs left over from the previous day. No one is entirely sure. And though various curry houses the length and breadth of Britain say the dish was their invention, none has an entirely convincing claim. What is clear is that its popularity is huge. And, although it is now available on menus in Asia, it is far more popular outside the Indian subcontinent than it is within it.

## BALTI

Britain has Birmingham to thank for the balti, a type of curry featuring marinated meat and vegetables cooked over a fast flame in a round-bottomed pot or wok, which is then served to the table sizzling in the container. The word balti is actually a name for the pot in which it is cooked and served. The spicy dish was introduced to Birmingham by its large Kashmiri population in the 1980s and many believe that the dish was actually invented by Kashmiris living in Britain. The *'Balti Triangle'* is an area in south Birmingham featuring a large number of restaurants that specialize in baltis. Brummies maintain that you can't get a proper balti outside the West Midlands.

# TRADITIONAL BRITISH FOOD

### Cream teas

Cream teas are particularly popular in tea rooms in Devon and Cornwall that cater to tourists and it is from this area of the country that cream teas originate. There is some evidence that cream teas were invented by monks in Tavistock at the turn of the 10th century, who prepared them for workers rebuilding the town's Benedictine abbey. Apparently they proved so popular that monks continued to serve them to passing travellers after the construction was finished.

## CORNISH PASTY

The Cornwall records office has a pasty recipe from 1746, but it is likely that the dish dates back further than that. A Cornish pasty is a type of pie containing steak, onion, potatoes and other ingredients that differ from pasty to pasty. It was invented for Cornish miners who weren't able to return to the surface for lunch. The idea was that the pasty contained a whole meal and one theory is that miners would eat the insides and then throw away the pastry, which would get dirty inside the mine.

### Things you may not know about the Cornish pasty

♦ *It is said that a good pasty should be strong enough to survive being dropped down a mine shaft.*

♦ It is bad luck for fishermen to take pasties to sea.

♦ *Miners' wives baked their husbands' initials into the crust so miners could tell them apart.*

♦ Some say that what makes a Cornish pasty unique is that all the ingredients should be cooked from raw.

♦ *A traditional Cornish tale says that the devil will never cross the River Tamar into Cornwall as he knows that Cornishwomen will put any available food inside pasties and is worried about ending up as a pasty filling.*

## The Sunday roast

A Sunday roast is the most British meal imaginable, comprising roasted meat and potatoes with vegetables, all smothered in gravy. It's not just a dish, but a tradition, dating back to the 18th century and thought to originate in Yorkshire. Families could put the meat in the oven before going to church on a Sunday morning, which would then be ready to eat when they returned home. Beef is the most British of roast meats, but chicken, lamb and pork are also hugely popular. Although meat is central to the meal, it's the trimmings and gravy that make it.

---

### HERE'S WHAT TRADITIONALLY GOES WITH WHAT

ROAST BEEF *Yorkshire pudding, horseradish sauce and English mustard* ⌘ ROAST PORK *crackling, sage and onion stuffing and apple sauce* ⌘ ROAST LAMB *mint sauce* ⌘ ROAST CHICKEN *stuffing, bread sauce, cranberry sauce*

---

### CHEDDAR

Cheddar is the most popular cheese in Britain, accounting for over 50 per cent of the country's total cheese market, worth £1.9 billion. Although it's now made all over the world, Cheddar cheese was invented in England and named after the region it originally came from.

• *King Henry II purchased 10,240 lbs of Cheddar in 1170 at a farthing per lb (that's 4,644 kg at a total cost of £10.67!).*

• When Charles I was on the throne, demand outweighed supply so much that you could only get Cheddar at the King's court, and even then you had to pay before the cheese was made.

• *Scott of the Antarctic took 3,500 lbs (nearly 1,600 kg) of Cheddar made in Cheddar on his famous expedition in 1901.*

• Originally cheese had to be made within 30 miles of Wells Cathedral to qualify for the name Cheddar.

Source: www.cheddargorgecheeseco.co.uk

In Yorkshire a pork pie is often called a *'growler'*. In the rest of Britain, growler is slang for something else.

## HP Sauce

Britain has a grocer from Nottingham called Frederick Gibson Garton to thank for HP Sauce. He invented the recipe and registered the name in 1896 before selling both to Edwin Samson Moore and the Midlands Vinegar Company, which launched the brown sauce in 1903. Rumour has it that HP stands for Harry Palmer, who originally came up with the idea before selling the recipe to Garton in repayment of a gambling debt. It's a nice story, but it's equally likely to be because the enterprising Garton heard that his sauce was being served in the Houses of Parliament, which have been pictured on the label ever since, and thought this could add to sales. Despite its ultra-patriotic image, HP Sauce moved production to Holland in 2007.

 In the 1960s and 1970s HP Sauce was known as 'Wilson's Gravy' after the Prime Minister, Harold Wilson. This was because in an interview with the *Sunday Times* his wife said, 'If Harold has a fault, it is that he will drown everything with HP Sauce.'

## Bovril

Invented in 1886 by Scotsman John Lawson Johnston to feed Napoleon's troops on the Russian front, Bovril was designed as a sort of liquid beef and called 'Johnston's Fluid Beef'. Two years later some 3,000 pubs were serving Bovril or 'beef tea' in Britain. Today, over 3 million jars of Bovril (enough to make 900 tons of beef tea) are sold per year.

 Custard is known as *crème anglaise* (meaning English sauce or English cream) by the French.

## FULL ENGLISH/SCOTTISH/WELSH BREAKFAST

All over Britain, the basic contents of a traditional breakfast are the same. It consists of sausages, bacon, fried or grilled tomatoes, fried mushrooms and baked beans accompanied by either toast, fried bread or bread and butter and brown sauce or ketchup. In the North it's also more likely to feature black pudding. Scottish variants include fried haggis, potato scones and oatcakes, while in Wales they often also serve it with 'laverbread'. This is a seaweed purée mixed with oatmeal and made into patties, before being fried in bacon fat.

*'There are certain things that you have to be British, or at least older than me, or possibly both, to appreciate: skiffle music, salt-cellars with a single hole, Marmite (an edible yeast extract with the visual properties of an industrial lubricant).'*
Bill Bryson, *Notes from a Small Island*

### MARMITE

'Love it or Hate it?' *The answer to Marmite's marketing slogan is something that polarizes the nation. Quite simply some Brits love the dark brown gooey paste, while others can't stand the stuff. First invented in 1902, Marmite predates the Australian Vegemite and Swiss Cenovis, which are simply imitations of the original. The savoury spread, which is made from yeast extract, is frequently cited as one of the most longed-for snacks by British expats. An article in* The Guardian *in 1994 describes how the first thing a British backpacker kidnapped in India by Kashmiri separatists did when he arrived back in Britain was to eat Marmite on toast. 'It was pretty good. It's just one of those things – you get out of the country and it's all you can think about,' he said.*

## THE FAGGOT

The reason Britain has such a bad reputation for cuisine abroad is because it gave birth to foodstuffs such as the faggot. A traditional dish in the southwest of England, Wales and the Black Country, the faggot is a meatball, made from unwanted off-cuts of meat and offal, wrapped in a 'caul', a membrane from the pig's abdomen. Faggots peaked during World War II when there wasn't much food around and have since plummeted in popularity.

## HAGGIS

Take the heart, liver and lungs of a sheep and chop it up. Then mix with onion, oatmeal, suet and spices, before stuffing this mixture inside an empty sheep's stomach and then boiling for hours. To some, this traditional Scottish dish sounds delicious, to others downright distasteful. It's not clear who invented the haggis (although it does have similarities with an Ancient Greek sausage), but Scots have been eating the stuff for centuries. Some believe it originates from farming folk from the Highlands needing a convenient food to transport, while others suggest it was a way of eating offal before it went off at the site of a hunt. Nowadays, it is traditionally eaten with *'neeps and tatties'* (turnips and potatoes) and washed down with whisky on Burns Night, which commemorates Scottish poet, Robert Burns. Many fish and chip shops in Scotland also offer a *'haggis supper'*, consisting of deep-fried haggis and chips.

 True Scots haggis is banned in the US as the law forbids the sale of animal lungs for human consumption. Americans don't know what they're missing out on.

The World Record for Haggis Hurling is held by Alan Pettigrew who threw a 1.5 lb haggis 180 feet, 10 inches in August 1984.

## Wild Haggis

'A haggis is a wee, three-legged Scottish Highland creature, with legs shorter on one side than the other so it can run fast around mountains.' This is the gist of a common reply to visitors to Scotland who ask, 'What is a haggis?' A group of haggis is called a heap, they lay Scotch eggs and are hunted during haggis season. The *Scotsman*'s website runs an annual Haggis Hunt. This may all sound ridiculous, but according to a survey by haggis manufacturers Hall's of Broxburn in 2003, a third of US visitors to Scotland believed the wild haggis to be a real creature.

## ADDRESS TO A HAGGIS

*Fair fa' your honest, sonsie face,*
*Great chieftain o' the puddin'-race!*
*Aboon them a' ye tak yer place,*
*Painch, tripe, or thairm:*
*Weel are ye wordy o' a grace*
*As lang's my airm.*

*The groaning trencher there ye fill,*
*Your hurdies like a distant hill,*
*Your pin wad help to mend a mill*
*In time o need,*

*While thro your pores the dews distil*
*Like amber bead.*

*His knife see rustic Labour dicht,*
*An cut you up wi ready slicht,*
*Trenching your gushing entrails bricht,*
*Like onie ditch;*
*And then, Oh what a glorious sicht,*
*Warm-reekin, rich!*

Robert Burns

# WHO INVENTED FISH AND CHIPS?

Although Brits didn't invent fish and chips, we did invent the modern-day fish and chip shop. It is thought that deep-fried fish was first introduced to Britain by Spanish and Portuguese Jews in the 16th and 17th centuries, while chipped potatoes grew in popularity in Europe following the introduction of the potato in the 17th century. Chip shops started to pop up in the North of England during the 19th century and Charles Dickens mentions a 'fried fish warehouse' in *Oliver Twist*, but Joseph Malin was perhaps the first to combine the two, opening Malin's which sold fried fish with chipped potatoes in London's East End in 1860.

---

## Fish facts

● Fish and chip shops in Britain sell more than 250 million portions of fish and chips each year.

● Fish and chip takeaways are four times more popular than Indian curries.

● Takeaway nation: nearly 70 per cent of Brits take their fish and chips home to eat.

● Cod is the most popular fish sold in fish and chip shops accounting for 61.5 per cent of fish sold, followed by haddock at 25 per cent.

● People in Yorkshire eat more fish and chips than anyone else in the country.

● One in six Brits goes to a fish and chip shop at least once a week.

● On a Friday, 20 per cent of meals in Britain are bought from a fish and chip shop.

● During World War II, fish and chips remained one of the few foods in the UK not subject to rationing.

● One in three British potatoes ends up in chips: that makes 2 million tonnes of chips every year.

● If you laid all the British potatoes that become chips each year end to end, the chip chain would stretch to the moon and back.

*Source: Sea Fish Industry Authority, The Potato Council*

## BRITAIN'S TOP CHIPPY

With more than 11,500 fish and chip shops in the UK, being named Britain's top chippy is no small feat. Each year since 1988, the Sea Fish Industry Authority awards one eaterie the honour of being *'Fish & Chip Shop of the Year'*. The following represent the best fish and chip shops in Britain:

2005  Hodgson's Chippy *Lancaster*

2004  Our Plaice *West Hagley*

2003  Finnegan's Fish Bar *Bridgend*

2002  Brownsover Fish Bar *Rugby*

2001  Allports Fish and Chip Shop *Pwllheli*

2000  Les's Fish Bar *Crewe*

1999  Bizzie Lizzies *Skipton*

1998  Zanre's *Peterhead*

1997  The Bervie Chipper *Inverbervie*

1996  Halfway Fish Bar *Poole*

1995  Hutchinson's *Helston*

1994  The West End Café *Rothesay*

1993  Reed Square Fish Bar *Birmingham*

1992  Elite Fish Bar & Restaurant *Ruskington*

1991  Chez Fred *Bournemouth*

1990  The Ashvale Fish Restaurant *Aberdeen*

1989  Skippers *Peterborough*

1988  Toffs of Muswell Hill *London*

---

### What's worse than mushy peas?

Particularly in the North of England, mushy peas are a popular accompaniment to fish and chips, but in Holyhead in North Wales the chip shops serve another pea-based side order. 'Peas Water' consists of the water strained from mushy peas and is given out free of charge. Mushy peas have enjoyed something of a renaissance in the past 15 years or so and some upmarket restaurants now feature them on their menus as 'Yorkshire Caviar'.

# THE BRITISH SEASIDE

Tourism in Britain probably began with medieval pilgrimages so it's no surprise that the word 'holiday' derives from 'holy day'. By the 18th century, health was the main reason for taking a holiday and spas were where the British public went in search of cures for gout, liver disorders and bronchitis, among other illnesses. By late Victorian times, huge numbers of people were taking advantage of better transport links and statutory days off to head for the seaside.

## Saucy postcards

Picture postcards were first allowed by the Royal Mail in 1894 and, by the 1930s, the British were sending 16 million a year. Donald McGill was the master of the saucy postcard, replete with flushed Brits in awkward situations giving rise to crude innuendo. The government tried to ban these cards in the 1950s, but now they are collectors' items.

## BLACKPOOL

Those who refer to Blackpool as the Las Vegas of Europe have clearly never been to Las Vegas. Aside from the lack of casinos, the cuisine is more fish and chips and seaside rock than all-you-can-eat buffets, the entertainment more Ken Dodd than Elvis and you're more likely to encounter an intoxicated bloke on a stag do wearing a *'Kiss-me-Quick'* trilby than a Texan billionaire in a ten-gallon hat. But the two do share similarities when it comes to tackiness, vulgarity and the opportunity to indulge in good- and not-so-good-natured debauchery. Blackpool is the home of the British *'dirty weekend'*. In the first half of the 20th century, it was frequently difficult to find a room as so many were occupied by a 'Mr and Mrs Smith'.

## Blackpool Tower

Designed as England's answer to the Eiffel Tower, Blackpool Tower is a hugely popular British tourist attraction. The 158-metre erection cost £42,000 to build, opened to the public in 1894 and nowadays features a circus, aquarium and ballroom, as well as a fish and chip shop. The Union Jack tends to fly from the top of the tower.

## PUNCH AND JUDY

Punch and Judy is weird. A puppet show centred around a violent, hook-nosed, hunchback who beats his wife and baby, while screaming, 'That's the way to do it!', in an irritating squawk, is not an obvious candidate for popular entertainment. But then shining a tongue-in-cheek light on a dysfunctional family is a comedic formula that persistently pays off: just look at *The Simpsons*. Considering its status as British seaside stalwart, it's strange to think that we have the Italians to thank for the Punch and Judy show. Mr Punch derives from 'Pulcinella', a stock character in 16th-century Italian comedy. Punch and Judy came into its own in Britain during the 19th century.

### MR PUNCH IN OTHER COUNTRIES

FRANCE *Polichinelle/Le Guignol* ◇ NETHERLANDS *Jan Klaassen* ◇ TURKEY *Karagoz* ◇ AUSTRIA *Kaspar* ◇ RUSSIA *Russia* ◇ GERMANY *Hans Wurst* ◇ ITALY *Pulcinella* ◇ ROMANIA *Vasilache* ◇ DENMARK *Mester Jackel*

 60-year-old Ronnie Alden was banned from performing his Punch and Judy show at a school in Shropshire in 2004 because it was deemed to be too violent.

# BRITISH SLANG

> **SLANG** n. informal language that is more common in speech than in writing and is typically restricted to a particular context or group

## THE FULL MONTY

Before the 1990s the term 'the full monty' was mainly in use in the North of England, but since then its popularity has spread throughout Britain, no doubt partly thanks to the popularity of the film of the same name. Here are some theories about the phrase's origin:

♦ A corruption of the phrase *'the full amount'*.

♦ A reference based on gambling jargon in which the Spanish for mountain, *monte*, means the entire pot or kitty.

♦ A reference to Field Marshal Montgomery's long-winded and comprehensive field briefings during World War II.

♦ A reference to the enormous collection of medals that adorned Montgomery's chest.

♦ A reference to Montgomery's penchant for a very large, full English breakfast before striding into battle.

♦ From the 1980s Del Monte fruit juice TV ad in which characters ask for *'the full del monte'*.

## YOU'RE FIRED

There is a theory that the slang term for being dismissed from your job comes from the practice of Scottish clans, whose members used to burn down the houses of people they no longer wanted as their clansfolk.

## GORDON BENNETT!!

'*Gordon Bennett*' is commonly used as an exclamation to indicate shock or surprise in Britain. It probably refers to an American and not a Brit at all, although his father was born in Scotland. Gordon Bennett was a 19th century playboy and newspaper mogul, whose exploits were so outrageous that his name became the popular way of expressing incredulity. Whether he was organizing balloon races, urinating in a fireplace in front of guests at a genteel New Year's Eve party, burning rolls of money or funding explorations, Gordon Bennett consistently surprised people. Another theory is that it is a politer way of exclaiming '*God*'.

### Some Yorkshire slang terms and colloquialisms

**a bad-un** a bad person ✻ **a bit-a'snap** snack ✻ **ah-reet kid** friendly greeting ✻ **any road** any way ✻ **'appen** perhaps ✻ **a rate gud so-art** good sort of person ✻ **babbie** baby ✻ **bairn** child ✻ **barmpot** a stupid person ✻ **beefing** crying ✻ **bewer** a good looking female ✻ **bins** glasses ✻ **black dag** black pudding ✻ **by 'eck** exclamation of astonishment ✻ **champion** really good ✻ **charver** chav ✻ **chuddy** chewing gum ✻ **chusty** big ✻ **eee an't got-a-clue** he has no idea ✻ **eeh-bah-gum** exclamation of astonishment ✻ **got-it back-uds** misunderstood the point ✻ **gruds** underpants ✻ **I don't gi' a chuff** I don't care ✻ **it caps owt** it beats everything ✻ **it's nut jannock** it's not fair ✻ **mardy** moody ✻ **nobbut a mention** not worth mentioning ✻ **nowt** nothing ✻ **owt** anything ✻ **owt for nowt** something for nothing ✻ **right/reet** very ✻ **splig** spider ✻ **steg** ugly female ✻ **ta'ra** goodbye ✻ **tha's nowt so-queer as folk** people can be strange ✻ **thou** you ✻ **twonk** idiot ✻ **wazzock** fool

## COCKNEY RHYMING SLANG

Although rhyming slang of sorts is heard all over Britain and indeed the English-speaking world, it is cockney rhyming slang that is the most infamous. Originating in London's East End, cockney rhyming slang started to become prominent during the 19th century. One theory is that it was originally adopted by the criminal classes as a sort of everyday code; another that, like any local dialect, it developed to confuse non-locals and foster a sense of community. Nowadays cockney rhyming slang is a sort of umbrella term for any rhyming slang used in Britain.

### CELEBRITY RHYMING SLANG

At the end of the 20th century it became common to relate rhyming slang to celebrities. Here're some examples:

AYRTON SENNA: *tenner* ◇ CLAIRE RAYNERS: *trainers* ◇ DARREN GOUGH: *cough* ◇ DAMON HILL: *pill* ◇ GARY ABLETT: *ecstasy tablet* ◇ GARY GLITTER: *shitter, meaning anus* ◇ GIANLUCA VIALLI: *Charlie, meaning cocaine* ◇ JACK DEE: *pee* ◇ JANET STREET-PORTER: *quarter, meaning a measurement of drugs* ◇ KATE MOSSED: *lost* ◇ BRITNEY SPEARS: *beers* ◇ PAUL WELLER: *Stella (Artois)* ◇ WALLACE AND GROMIT: *vomit*

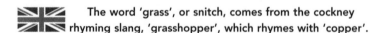

**The word 'grass', or snitch, comes from the cockney rhyming slang, 'grasshopper', which rhymes with 'copper'.**

•

**The US version of the** *Lock, Stock and Two Smoking Barrels* **DVD contains a glossary of cockney rhyming slang to help 'septic tanks' (Yanks) decipher what the characters are talking about.**

# THE ENGLISH LANGUAGE

The English language is one of the most colourful and widely spoken languages in the world. It may have been invented in Britain, but it's something of a mongrel, incorporating words and phrases from more than 100 other languages. Thanks in great part to the British Empire it has spread far beyond the British Isles. It's estimated to be the first language of some 380 million people and the second language of approximately 600 million. Interestingly, although the vast majority of the population speaks and writes English, Britain has no *'official'* language.

---

### 'Nosey' Parker

It's thanks to a 16th-century Archbishop of Canterbury that the term 'nosey parker' entered the English language as a means of describing someone overly concerned with the business of others. Matthew Parker was supposedly a shy and retiring man in most matters, but was intensely inquisitive about church affairs. It was this that led his enemies and critics to refer to him as Nosey Parker and not the size of his nose.

---

### OLD NOSEY

The Duke of Wellington was supposed to have possessed an incredibly large nose and many of his soldiers nicknamed him *'Old Nosey'*. Legend has it that during the Peninsular War a sentry challenged Wellington who had forgotten the day's password. The sentry, however, remembered his senior's nose. *'God bless your crooked nose, sir. I would rather see it than 10,000 men,'* the sentry is alleged to have said.

# WORDS AND PHRASES IN THE ENGLISH LANGUAGE THAT COME FROM THE FRENCH

*brasserie ♦ nom de plume ♦ joie de vivre ♦ soirée ♦ faux pas ♦ savoir-faire ♦ nouveau riche ♦ mon dieu ♦ haute couture ♦ canapé ♦ consommé ♦ purée ♦ laissez-faire ♦ panache*

---

## Foreign origins of some words in the English language

• CHECKMATE comes from the Persian phrase, *shah mat,* meaning *'the king is dead'*.

• ADMIRAL is from the Arabic phrase, *amir al bahr*, meaning *'lord of the sea'*.

• BEELZEBUB is a name for the devil, which comes from the Hebrew for *'lord of the flies'*.

• PARIAH, meaning *outcast*, originates from the untouchable caste, *Pariyan*, in India.

• SHAMPOO comes from the Hindi word, *champna*, for *'press'*.

• PUNCH the drink comes from the Indian word, *pancham*, meaning *five* in Sanskrit and is described as a drink with five ingredients.

• CATAMARAN derives from the Tamil word, *kattumaaram*, meaning logs tied together.

• CURRY comes from the Tamil word *'kari'* meaning spiced sauce.

• DINGHY comes from the Hindi words *dingi* or *dengi* for small boat.

• CORDUROY comes from the French *cord du roi* or *'cloth of the king'*.

• AVERAGE comes from the Arabic, *awariyah*, meaning damaged goods.

• COTTON derives from the Arabic word *qutun*.

• SAFFRON comes from the Arabic word *zafaran*.

• ARTICHOKE comes from the Arabic word *al kharshuf*.

• BUFFOON comes from the Italian word, *buffone*, for clown.

• BANKRUPT derives from the Italian phrase *banca rotta*, meaning *'broken bench'*.

• YACHT comes from the Dutch, *yacht*, meaning *'hunting ship'*.

• ROBOT comes from the Czech *robata*, meaning *'compulsory service'*.

## THANKS, VISHNU

The Hindu God, Vishnu, has contributed two words to English: *'avatar'* meaning incarnation, referring to his 10 incarnations on Earth and *'juggernaut'* meaning a massive, unstoppable force, which comes from one of the names with which Vishnu is worshipped.

## LINGUISTIC MISCELLANY

♦ The following sentence contains nine ways in which *'ough'* can be pronounced:

*'A rough-coated, dough-faced, thoughtful ploughman strode through the streets of Scarborough; after falling into a slough, he coughed and hiccoughed.'*

♦ *'bookkeeper'* and *'bookkeeping'* are the only words in the English language with three consecutive double letters.

♦ The only 15-letter word that can be spelled without repeating a letter is *'uncopyrightable'*.

♦ If you speak English, you know parts of at least a hundred different languages.

♦ The word *'set'* has more definitions than any other word in the English language.

♦ The verb *'cleave'* is the only English word with two synonyms which are antonyms of each other: *adhere* and *separate.*

♦ According to James Bartlett, the highest-scoring word in the English language game of Scrabble is *'quartzy'*. This will score 164 points if played across a red triple-word square with the Z on a light blue double-letter square.

♦ The English word with the most consonants in a row is *'latchstring'*.

♦ No other words in the English language rhyme with orange, silver or purple.

♦ The sentence, *'The quick brown fox jumps over the lazy dog'*, uses every letter in the alphabet.

♦ *'The apple of his eye'*, *'a labour of love'* and *'by the skin of his teeth'* are all phrases that derive from the King James Bible.

**Freelance** This word comes from a medieval term referring to a knight who was not pledged to one master and therefore possessed a lance which was free for hire.

**Rule of thumb** One theory is that this phrase derives from an old English law which stated that you couldn't beat your wife with anything wider than your thumb. Another is that it comes from carpenters who used the length of the first joint of the thumb, which is about an inch, to measure things.

**Second string** This phrase, which refers to a replacement or back-up comes from the Middle Ages, when an archer always carried a second string in case the one on his bow broke.

**Sleep tight** Derives from the fact that early mattresses were filled with straw and held up with rope stretched across the bedframe; a tight sleep, therefore, was a comfortable sleep.

**One for the road** During the Middle Ages, the condemned were often transported from cells in London to Tyburn Hill for execution. Along the route they would stop and allow the condemned to have one final drink on the way to death.

**Mind your Ps and Qs** Ale used to be drunk in pints and quarts and, when drunken customers got unruly and out of hand, sensible landlords would often suggest customers should mind their own pints and quarts, or ps and qs, and settle down.

## Why is pound abbreviated to 'lb'?

It comes from the Latin, *libra ponda*, meaning *weight* or *balance*. This is also where the star sign gets its name from.

*pneumonoultramicroscopicsilicovolcanoconiosis* is a lung disease and also the longest English word ever to appear in an English dictionary.

# WILLIAM SHAKESPEARE

### THE WORLD'S GREATEST WRITER

The most-quoted writer in the history of English literature was born in the year 1564 in Stratford-upon-Avon and wrote at least 37 plays and 154 sonnets during his lifetime. The lack of solid information about Shakespeare's life has led to various speculations about the person behind the poet and playwright. At some point or another, his sexuality, his politics, his religion, his marital status and even his true identity have all been questioned. What isn't in question is the quality and breadth of the work. While criticizing him in an essay, even his peer Ben Jonson admits that Shakespeare's plays are *'not of an age, but for all time'*. Among others, Sir Francis Bacon, Christopher Marlowe, the poet Phillip Sydney and the 17th Earl of Oxford, Edward de Vere have all been suggested as the true author of the Shakespeareian works. But, although there is some evidence that there may have been collaboration, the idea that William Shakespeare was merely a pseudonym is unlikely. And, Britain can be rightly proud of producing the world's greatest writer.

## 11 well-known Shakespeareian quotes

- To be or not to be, that is the question...
- O Romeo, Romeo! wherefore art thou Romeo?
- All the world's a stage...
- The lady doth protest too much, methinks
- Is this a dagger which I see before me?
- Off with his head!
- The course of true love never did run smooth
- What a piece of work is man!
- My words fly up, my thoughts remain below
- Now is the winter of our discontent
- Frailty, thy name is woman!

## COMMON MISQUOTES

• MISQUOTE: *There is method in this madness*
TRUE QUOTE: *Though this be madness, yet there is method in 't*

• MISQUOTE: *Alas, poor Yorick! I knew him well*
TRUE QUOTE: *Alas, poor Yorick! I knew him, Horatio*

• MISQUOTE: *All that glistens is not gold*
TRUE QUOTE: *All that glisters is not gold*

• MISQUOTE: *We are such stuff... As dreams are made of*
TRUE QUOTE: *We are such stuff... As dreams are made on*

### Eight Shakespearean oddities

❋ Shakespeare shares his birthday with St George, the patron saint of England.

❋ *No known direct descendants of Shakespeare are alive today.*

❋ As an actor, Shakespeare is thought to have played the part of the ghost in *Hamlet*.

❋ *One account suggests that Shakespeare died after a night's heavy drinking with fellow playwrights Ben Jonson and Michael Drayton.*

❋ Shakespeare invented the word 'assassination'.

❋ *His plays may be studied in universities the world over, but Shakespeare is thought to have left school at the age of 15 and never attended university.*

❋ Suicides or suspected suicides occur an unlucky 13 times in Shakespeare's plays. (Once in *Romeo and Juliet*, *Othello*, *Hamlet* and *Macbeth*, three times in *Julius Caesar* and five times in *Antony and Cleopatra*.)

❋ *There is circumstantial evidence that William Shakespeare's father could neither read nor write.*

**Shakespeare's father briefly worked as an ale-taster or 'beer-conner', as it was known in the borough of Stratford, during the 1550s.**

## SHAKESPEARE'S PLAYS

### COMEDIES

ALL'S WELL THAT ENDS WELL ◇ AS YOU LIKE IT ◇ THE COMEDY OF ERRORS ◇ CYMBELINE ◇ LOVE'S LABOURS LOST ◇ MEASURE FOR MEASURE ◇ THE MERRY WIVES OF WINDSOR ◇ THE MERCHANT OF VENICE ◇ A MIDSUMMER NIGHT'S DREAM ◇ MUCH ADO ABOUT NOTHING ◇ PERICLES, PRINCE OF TYRE ◇ TAMING OF THE SHREW ◇ THE TEMPEST ◇ TROILUS AND CRESSIDA ◇ TWELFTH NIGHT ◇ TWO GENTLEMEN OF VERONA ◇ WINTER'S TALE

### HISTORIES

HENRY IV, PART I ◇ HENRY IV, PART II ◇ HENRY V ◇ HENRY VI, PART I ◇ HENRY VI, PART II ◇ HENRY VI, PART III ◇ HENRY VIII ◇ KING JOHN ◇ RICHARD II ◇ RICHARD III

### TRAGEDIES

ANTONY AND CLEOPATRA ◇ CORIOLANUS ◇ HAMLET ◇ JULIUS CAESAR ◇ KING LEAR ◇ MACBETH ◇ OTHELLO ◇ ROMEO AND JULIET ◇ TIMON OF ATHENS ◇ TITUS ANDRONICUS

### The lost play

There is some evidence that Shakespeare wrote another play called *Cardenio* in his lifetime, which has been lost since Shakespeare's death. There is no known written record of it in existence today.

> *Good friend for Jesus sake forbeare*
> *To digg the dust encloased heare*
> *Blessed by y man y spares hes stones*
> *And curst be he y moves my bones*
> The epitaph inscribed on Shakespeare's tombstone

# BOOKS AND WRITERS

## THE LIBRARY LAW

By law the British Library must be given a copy of every work published in the UK and Ireland within a month of publication. The following five libraries can request a free copy:

BODLEIAN LIBRARY, OXFORD ❖ THE UNIVERSITY LIBRARY, CAMBRIDGE ❖ THE NATIONAL LIBRARY OF SCOTLAND, EDINBURGH ❖ THE LIBRARY OF TRINITY COLLEGE, DUBLIN ❖ THE NATIONAL LIBRARY OF WALES, ABERYSTWYTH

The Copyright Act 1911 and the Irish Copyright Act 1963

## NOBEL PRIZE IN LITERATURE WINNERS FROM BRITAIN

**2005** – HAROLD PINTER *'who in his plays uncovers the precipice under everyday prattle and forces entry into oppression's closed rooms'*

**2001** – V.S. NAIPAUL *'for having united perceptive narrative and incorruptible scrutiny in works that compel us to see the presence of suppressed histories'*

**1983** – WILLIAM GOLDING *'for his novels which, with the perspicuity of realistic narrative art and the diversity and universality of myth, illuminate the human condition in the world of today'*

**1981** – ELIAS CANETTI *'for writings marked by a broad outlook, a wealth of ideas and artistic power'*

**1953** – WINSTON CHURCHILL *'for his brilliant oratory in defending exalted human values'*

**1950** – BERTRAND RUSSELL *'in recognition of his varied and significant writings in which he champions humanitarian ideals and freedom of thought'*

**1948** – T.S. ELIOT *'for his outstanding, pioneer contribution to present-day poetry'*

**1932** – JOHN GALSWORTHY *'for his distinguished art of narration which takes its highest form in* The Forsyte Saga*'*

**1907** – RUDYARD KIPLING *'in consideration of the power of observation, originality of imagination, virility of ideas and remarkable talent for narration which characterize the creations of this world-famous author'*

Source: www.nobleprize.org

## Booker Prize winners from Britain

The Man Booker Prize for Fiction, or Booker Prize as it is better known, is awarded each year for the best novel written in English by a citizen of the Commonwealth of Nations or the Republic of Ireland.

| | | |
|---|---|---|
| **2004** | Alan Hollinghurst | *The Line of Beauty* |
| **1998** | Ian McEwan | *Amsterdam* |
| **1996** | Graham Swift | *Last Orders* |
| **1995** | Pat Barker | *The Ghost Road* |
| **1994** | James Kelman | *How Late It Was, How Late* |
| **1992** | Barry Unsworth | *Sacred Hunger* |
| **1990** | A.S. Byatt | *Possession: A Romance* |
| **1987** | Penelope Lively | *Moon Tiger* |
| **1986** | Kingsley Amis | *The Old Devils* |
| **1984** | Anita Brookner | *Hotel du Lac* |
| **1980** | William Golding | *Rites of Passage* |
| **1979** | Penelope Fitzgerald | *Offshore* |
| **1978** | Iris Murdoch | *The Sea, the Sea* |
| **1977** | Paul Scott | *Staying On* |
| **1976** | David Storey | *Saville* |
| **1975** | Ruth Prawer Jhabvala | *Heat and Dust* |
| **1974** | Stanley Middleton | *Holiday* |
| **1973** | J.G. Farrell | *The Siege of Krishnapur* |
| **1972** | John Berger | *G* |
| **1971** | V.S. Naipaul | *In a Free State* |
| **1970** | Bernice Rubens | *The Elected Member* |
| **1969** | P.H. Newby | *Something to Answer For* |

 In 1998, a William Caxton edition of *The Canterbury Tales* (1476) sold at auction for a then world record price of £4.2 million.

## POETS LAUREATE

Created by royal appointment, the Poet Laureate is expected to compose poetry for state occasions and important national events.

| | |
|---|---|
| 1730–57 | *Colley Cibber* |
| 1757–85 | *William Whitehead* |
| 1785–90 | *Thomas Warton* |
| 1790–1813 | *Henry James Pye* |
| 1813–43 | *Robert Southey* |
| 1843–50 | *William Wordsworth* |
| 1850–92 | *Alfred Lord Tennyson* |
| 1896–1913 | *Alfred Austin* |
| 1913–30 | *Robert Bridges* |
| 1930–67 | *John Masefield* |
| 1968–72 | *Cecil Day-Lewis* |
| 1972–84 | *Sir John Betjeman* |
| 1984–98 | *Ted Hughes* |
| 1999 | *Andrew Motion* |

| | |
|---|---|
| 1668–89 | *John Dryden* |
| 1689–92 | *Thomas Shadwell* |
| 1692–1715 | *Nahum Tate* |
| 1715–18 | *Nicholas Rowe* |
| 1718–30 | *Laurence Eusden* |

### The Scots Makar

In 2004, Scotland appointed its first national poet, Edwin Morgan, known as the *'Scots Makar'*. The title is held for a period of three years and the position carries no specific salary or financial reward. The Scottish government plans to make it a traditional position. According to the Scottish Executive, *'The obligations of the holder, in general, would be to represent Scottish poetry in the public consciousness, to promote poetic creativity in Scotland, and to be an ambassador for Scottish poetry.'*

## THE ENGLISH NOVEL

The following have each been claimed to be the first English novel:

THOMAS MALORY, *Le Morte d'Arthur*, (1485) ◇ JOHN LYLY, *Euphues: The Anatomy of Wit* (1578) ◇ PHILIP SIDNEY, *The Countess of Pembroke's Arcadia* (1581) ◇ JOHN BUNYAN, *The Pilgrim's Progress* (1678) ◇ APHRA BEHN, *Oroonoko* (1688) ◇ DANIEL DEFOE, *Robinson Crusoe* (1719) ◇ DANIEL DEFOE, *Moll Flanders* (1722) ◇ SAMUEL RICHARDSON, *Pamela* (1740)

---

### The Big Read

In 2003 the BBC carried out a national survey to identify the 'Nation's Best-loved Book'. The top 10 were as follows:

**1** The Lord of the Rings by *J.R.R. Tolkien* **2** Pride and Prejudice by *Jane Austen* **3** His Dark Materials by *Philip Pullman* **4** The Hitchhiker's Guide to the Galaxy by *Douglas Adams* **5** Harry Potter and the Goblet of Fire by *J.K. Rowling* **6** To Kill a Mockingbird by *Harper Lee* **7** Winnie-the-Pooh by *A.A. Milne* **8** Nineteen Eighty-Four by *George Orwell* **9** The Lion, the Witch and the Wardrobe by *C.S. Lewis* **10** Jane Eyre by *Charlotte Brontë*

---

By 2006, author J.K. Rowling had sold over 377 million copies of the Harry Potter series. The first book, *Harry Potter and the Philosopher's Stone*, was turned down by no fewer than 12 publishing houses.

# HOW OLD IS OXFORD?

Although it's generally accepted that Oxford University is the oldest university in the English-speaking world, no one is quite sure when it was founded. It was definitely around at the end of the 11th century, but tracing its roots back further proves difficult.

---

### FAMOUS ALUMNI

Many famous and influential people have studied at Oxford including 25 British Prime Ministers, four British kings, 47 Nobel prize-winners, seven saints, 86 archbishops, 18 cardinals and one pope. Here's a selection of some of the famous people who studied there:

STEPHEN HAWKING ◇ TIM BERNERS-LEE ◇ HUGH GRANT ◇ KATE BECKINSALE ◇ MICHAEL PALIN ◇ KEN LOACH ◇ LAWRENCE OF ARABIA ◇ SIR WALTER RALEIGH ◇ RUPERT MURDOCH

Cambridge doesn't have quite the same political heritage as Oxford, but a lot of truly influential and famous Brits have studied there. Here's a selection:

OLIVER CROMWELL ◇ CHARLES DARWIN ◇ GERMAINE GREER ◇ STEPHEN HAWKING ◇ WILLIAM PITT THE YOUNGER ◇ ISAAC NEWTON ◇ EMMA THOMPSON ◇ JOHN MAYNARD KEYNES ◇ CHARLES, PRINCE OF WALES ◇ JOHN CLEESE ◇ CHARLES BABBAGE

---

 **Oxford's motto is** *Dominus Illuminatio Mea*, **which means** *'The Lord is my Light'* **and is taken from a psalm from the Bible.**

Oxford has the shortest terms of any British university; each is just eight weeks long. They are known as *Michaelmas* (Oct to Dec), *Hilary* (Jan to Mar) and *Trinity* (Apr to Jun).

## SOME WRITERS WHO STUDIED OR TAUGHT AT OXFORD

EVELYN WAUGH ◇ LEWIS CARROLL ◇ ALDOUS HUXLEY ◇ OSCAR WILDE ◇ C.S. LEWIS ◇ J.R.R. TOLKIEN ◇ PHILLIP PULLMAN ◇ VIKRAM SETH ◇ PLUM SYKES ◇ PERCY BYSSHE SHELLEY ◇ JOHN DONNE ◇ W. H. AUDEN ◇ PHILIP LARKIN ◇ CECIL DAY-LEWIS ◇ SIR JOHN BETJEMAN ◇ ANDREW MOTION

## SOME WRITERS WHO STUDIED OR TAUGHT AT CAMBRIDGE

LORD BYRON ◇ SAMUEL TAYLOR COLERIDGE ◇ TED HUGHES ◇ SIEGFRIED SASSOON ◇ BERTRAND RUSSELL ◇ SALMAN RUSHDIE ◇ SYLVIA PLATH ◇ A. A. MILNE ◇ JOHN MILTON ◇ VLADIMIR NABOKOV ◇ CHRISTOPHER MARLOWE ◇ TENNYSON ◇ WORDSWORTH

### OXFORD–CAMBRIDGE RIVALRY

The rivalry between the two universities dates back to the time when Cambridge was formed by dissident scholars from Oxford. The most high-profile example of the competitiveness between the pair these days is the annual Oxford–Cambridge boat race, but almost all sports from rugby to tiddlywinks have what's known as an annual *'Varsity'* match where the two universities compete against each other.

Until 1866 one had to belong to the Church of England to receive a BA degree from Oxford, while until 1920 one had to have knowledge of Ancient Greek and, until 1960, knowledge of Latin.

•

Lawrence of Arabia was both a student and a don at Oxford.

## The colleges

OXFORD BOASTS 39 COLLEGES IN ALL

| Name | Founded | Name | Founded |
| --- | --- | --- | --- |
| All Souls College | 1438 | Nuffield College | 1937 |
| Balliol College | 1263 | Oriel College | 1326 |
| Brasenose College | 1509 | Pembroke College | 1624 |
| Christ Church | 1546 | The Queen's College | 1341 |
| Corpus Christi College | 1517 | St Anne's College | 1878 |
| Exeter College | 1314 | St Antony's College | 1950 |
| Green College | 1979 | St Catherine's College | 1963 |
| Harris Manchester College | 1786 | St Cross College | 1965 |
| Hertford College | 1282 | St Edmund Hall | 1226 |
| Jesus College | 1571 | St Hilda's College | 1893 |
| Keble College | 1870 | St Hugh's College | 1886 |
| Kellogg College | 1990 | St John's College | 1555 |
| Lady Margaret Hall | 1878 | St Peter's College | 1929 |
| Linacre College | 1962 | Somerville College | 1879 |
| Lincoln College | 1427 | Templeton College | 1965 |
| Magdalen College | 1458 | Trinity College | 1554 |
| Mansfield College | 1886 | University College | 1249 |
| Merton College | 1264 | Wadham College | 1610 |
| New College | 1379 | Wolfson College | 1966 |
| | | Worcester College | 1714 |

## The colleges

CAMBRIDGE CONSISTS OF 31 COLLEGES IN ALL

| Name | Founded | Name | Founded |
|---|---|---|---|
| Christ's | 1505 | Magdalene | 1428 |
| Churchill | 1960 | New Hall | 1954 |
| Clare | 1326 | Newnham | 1871 |
| Clare Hall | 1965 | Pembroke | 1347 |
| Corpus Christi | 1352 | Peterhouse | 1284 |
| Darwin | 1964 | Queens' | 1448 |
| Downing | 1800 | Robinson | 1977 |
| Emmanuel | 1584 | St Catharine's | 1473 |
| Fitzwilliam | 1966 | St Edmund's | 1896 |
| Girton | 1869 | St John's | 1511 |
| Gonville and Caius | 1348 | Selwyn | 1882 |
| Homerton | 1976 | Sidney Sussex | 1596 |
| Hughes Hall | 1885 | Trinity | 1546 |
| Jesus | 1496 | Trinity Hall | 1350 |
| King's | 1441 | Wolfson | 1965 |
| Lucy Cavendish | 1965 | | |

## THE CAMBRIDGE WOODEN SPOON

A wooden spoon used to be awarded to the student with the lowest passing grade in the final Maths examinations. The last of these spoons was awarded to a student who was also a rower in 1909. It was over one metre in length and had an oar blade for a handle.

 Seven of the 11 prime ministers up to and including Tony Blair studied at Oxford.

## THE BBC

Founded in 1922, the BBC claims to be the largest broadcasting corporation in the world in terms of audience numbers. It's primarily funded by the British public via television licence fees, although it does bring in some commercial revenue by other means and through the BBC World Service, which is financed by the Foreign Office. Around the world the BBC is famed for its integrity, honesty and the quality of its journalism. In Britain these days, it's mainly famous for its continued commitment to commissioning cutting-edge comedy, from *Monty Python's Flying Circus* to *Little Britain* and broadcasting Eastenders on a weekly basis. Its nicknames include the *'Beeb'* (which was coined by Kenny Everett) and *'Auntie'* (from a perceived *'Auntie knows best'* stance).

---

 **Until 1955, the BBC was the only television broadcaster in Britain.**

---

### THE WATERSHED

*'From 9pm the TV watershed helps parents protect children from unsuitable material. In all but exceptional circumstances, programmes before 9pm are suitable for general audiences including children. From 9pm they are progressively suitable only for adults. Because children's sensibilities vary as widely as those of adults, parents are expected to share responsibility in judging whether children should watch after 9pm. The BBC can be received in every household, but two-thirds of them have no children. Our public obligation is to provide services for all licence-payers as well as those with children.'*

The BBC's watershed policy • Source: BBC

---

### Where does the licence fee go?

In its 2005–2006 financial report the BBC broke down the average monthly licence fee spend as follows:

| | | | |
|---|---|---|---|
| BBC ONE | £3.52 | Digital television channels | £1.00 |
| BBC TWO | £1.52 | Local and Nations' radio | 68p |
| Transmission and collection costs | £1.08 | bbc.co.uk | 36p |
| | | BBC jam | 14p |
| Nations and English Regions television | £1.04 | Digital radio stations | 10p |
| | | Interactive TV (BBCi) | 8p |
| BBC Radio 1, 2, 3, 4 and Five Live | £1.02 | **Total** | **£10.54** |

## THE ARCHERS

The world's longest running radio soap is the everyday story of country folk in the fictional village of Ambridge. When it was first broadcast, *The Archers* had a remit to educate as well as entertain and the Ministry of Agriculture was involved in the direction of content. The brief was to help productivity in postwar Britain and reinforce notions of Englishness, while the country was rebuilt. Farmers and smallholders were supposed to tune in and learn. Before government involvement ended in 1972, the dialogue featured far more factual information about farming than is usual. These days, storylines are still about the price of cattle, rural class tension and bad weather, alongside tales of illicit affairs, drug abuse and gay marriage. Since 1951, more than 15,000 episodes have gone out.

---

 In 1994, the BBC World Service launched an Afghan soap opera called *New Home, New Life*, which was based on *The Archers*.

# CLASSIC BRITISH TV

### *Monty Python's Flying Circus*

Depicting a surreal world featuring spam, cross-dressing lumberjacks, absurd animation and a ministry of silly walks, Monty Python is one of the most influential comedy collectives of all time. The dead parrot sketch in which a customer and pet shop owner argue over the state of a 'Norwegian Blue' parrot is probably the most famous comedy skit in the history of television comedy. Michael Palin and Terry Jones met at Oxford University, while Graham Chapman, John Cleese and Eric Idle first encountered each other at Cambridge. The final member of the troupe, Terry Gilliam, is the only non-Brit in Monty Python and was born in Minnesota.

### FAMOUS LINES

*'Nobody expects the Spanish Inquisition!'*

\*

*'It's not pinin', it's passed on. This parrot is no more. It has ceased to be. It's expired and gone to meet its maker. This is a late parrot. It's a stiff. Bereft of life, it rests in peace. If you hadn't nailed it to the perch, it would be pushing up the daisies. It's rung down the curtain and joined the choir invisible. This is an ex-parrot.'*

\*

*'We use only the finest baby frogs, dew-picked and flown from Iraq, cleansed in finest-quality spring water, lightly killed, and then sealed in a succulent Swiss quintuple smooth treble cream milk chocolate envelope and lovingly frosted with glucose.'*

---

### Other names considered instead of *Monty Python's Flying Circus*

*Owl Stretching Time* ☺ *The Toad Elevating Moment* ☺ *Vaseline Review* ☺ *Bun, Wackett, Buzzard, Stubble and Boot*

## THE MONTY PYTHON FILM OEUVRE

*Monty Python's Flying Circus* (1969-1974) ◇ *And Now For Something Completely Different* (1971) ◇ *Monty Python and the Holy Grail* (1975) ◇ *Monty Python's Life of Brian* (1979) ◇ *The Meaning of Life* (1983)

## THE MONTY PYTHON LEGACY

• A gigantic prehistoric snake *Montypythonoides riversleighensis* was so called by the Australian palaeontologist and Python fan who discovered the fossil.

• Each Monty Python member has an asteroid named after him: *9617 Grahamchapman, 9618 Johncleese, 9619 Terrygilliam, 9620 Ericidle, 9621 Michaelpalin* and *9622 Terryjones.*

• Ben & Jerry's introduced a new ice cream flavour in 2006. *'Vermonty Python'* is a coffee liqueur ice cream featuring chocolate cookie crumb swirls and fudge cows.

• Nerds who developed the Python programming language named it after Monty Python, designed to reflect the idea that programming should be fun.

### Britain's Best Sitcom

During 2003–2004, the BBC conducted a poll to pick Britain's Best Sitcom. *Only Fools and Horses* won, but the BBC was criticized when it emerged that the top 10 sitcoms were all produced by the BBC. Here are the top 20:

*Only Fools and Horses* ♦ *Blackadder* ♦ *The Vicar of Dibley* ♦ *Dad's Army* ♦ *Fawlty Towers* ♦ *Yes Minister* ♦ *Porridge* ♦ *Open All Hours* ♦ *The Good Life* ♦ *One Foot in the Grave* ♦ *Father Ted* ♦ *Keeping Up Appearances* ♦ *'Allo 'Allo!* ♦ *Last of the Summer Wine* ♦ *Steptoe and Son* ♦ *Men Behaving Badly* ♦ *Absolutely Fabulous* ♦ *Red Dwarf* ♦ *The Royle Family* ♦ *Are You Being Served?*

## Doctor Whos

**1**st Doctor, played by William Hartnell (1963–1966) **2**nd Doctor, played by Patrick Troughton (1966–1969) **3**rd Doctor, played by Jon Pertwee (1970–1974) **4**th Doctor, played by Tom Baker (1974–1981) **5**th Doctor, played by Peter Davison (1981–1984) **6**th Doctor, played by Colin Baker (1984–1986) **7**th Doctor, played by Sylvester McCoy (1987–1989, 1996) **8**th Doctor, played by Paul McGann (1996) **9**th Doctor, played by Christopher Eccleston (2005) **10**th Doctor, played by David Tennant (2005–present)

## ONLY FOOLS AND HORSES

There has probably never been a TV show as beloved of Brits as *Only Fools and Horses*. Here's a list of some of the characters:

**Del Boy** *(Played by David Jason)* Archetypal market trader, who alongside his brother Rodney was the star of the show. A loveable loser with a number of catchphrases, 'You plonker, Rodney,' being perhaps the best known.

**Rodney** *(Nicholas Lyndhurst)* The straight man to the comical Del Boy.

**Grandad** *(Lennard Pearce)* Stereotypical pensioner who never took off his hat, even in bed.

**Uncle Albert** *(Buster Merryfield)* When Lennard Pearce (Grandad) died suddenly of a heart attack in 1984, the scriptwriters invented Uncle Albert, to basically play the same role.

**Trigger** *(Roger Lloyd Pack)* Local road sweeper and moron, who always refers to Rodney as 'Dave' and is known as Trigger because he looks like a horse.

**Boycie** *(John Challis)* With a trademark sneer of a voice and a machine-gun laugh, Boycie is supposed to be the character the audience loves to hate. Although more financially successful than Del Boy, it is the latter who always has the last laugh.

**Cassandra** *(Gwyneth Strong)* Rodney's eventual wife who looked worryingly like her husband.

**The first episode of *Doctor Who* was broadcast the day after John F Kennedy's assassination.**

## TOP SOAP

*EastEnders* is the BBC's flagship soap opera with primetime half-hour programmes four times a week. Its characters live and work around Albert Square in a fictional area of London's East End known as Walford in the postal district of E20 (the highest any real east London postal district goes is E18). The cast of stock characters in *EastEnders* lurch from crisis to crisis, then in extremis pull together, generally under the banner of family – 'You're a Mitchell!'. Arguably less humorous than its northern rival *Coronation Street*, *EastEnders* is filmed six to seven weeks ahead of broadcast and is then provided with topical inserts from time to time, so its cast are seen enjoying such important events as the World Cup at the same time as the audience.

## LITTLE BRITAIN

*Little Britain* began on Radio 4 in 2001 and transferred to TV in 2003. The opening voiceovers are absurd summaries of the nation's character: 'Britain... We've had running water for over 10 years, an underground tunnel linking us to Peru, and we invented the cat' or, 'Unlike other countries, Britain has people of two genders: women and men.'

### LITTLE BRITAIN CATCHPHRASES

VICKY POLLARD: *'Yeah but no but yeah ... don't go giving me evils.'*

DAFFYD THOMAS: *'I am the only gay in the village.'*

BUBBLES DE VERE: *'Call me Bubbles ... everyone does.'*

LOU: *'I want that one.'*

EMILY HOWARD: *'I am a lady.'*

CAROL BEER: *'Computer says no.'* *[Cough]*

## TOP 20 RATED TV SHOWS IN BRITAIN

**1** 1966 WORLD CUP FINAL *1966 BBC/ITV 32.30m* **2** FUNERAL OF PRINCESS DIANA *1997 BBC1/ITV 32.10m* **3** ROYAL FAMILY DOCUMENTARY *1969 BBC1/ITV 30.69m* **4** EASTENDERS: DEN DIVORCES ANGIE *1986 BBC1 30.15m* **5** APOLLO 13 SPLASHDOWN *1970 BBC1/ITV 28.6m* **6** FA CUP REPLAY: CHELSEA V LEEDS *1970 BBC1/ITV 28.49m* **7** ROYAL WEDDING: CHARLES AND DIANA *1981 BBC/ITV 28.40m* **8** PRINCESS ANNE'S WEDDING *1973 BBC1 27.60m* **9** CORONATION STREET: ALAN BRADLEY KILLED BY TRAM *1989 ITV 26.93m* **10** ONLY FOOLS AND HORSES: BATMAN AND ROBIN *1996 BBC1 24.35m* **11** EASTENDERS: PAT BUTCHER RUNS DOWN LITTLE GIRL *1992 BBC1 24.30m* **12** ROYAL VARIETY PERFORMANCE: SHIRLEY BASSEY, PETER COOK AND DUDLEY MOORE *1965 ITV 24.20m* **13** JFK ASSASSINATION NEWS *1963 BBC/ITV 24.15m* **14** WINTER OLYMPICS: TORVILL AND DEAN *1994 BBC1 23.95m* **15** TO THE MANOR BORN: PENELOPE KEITH HOLDS HANDS WITH PETER BOWLES *1979 BBC1 23.95m* **16** WORLD CUP: ENGLAND V ARGENTINA *1998 ITV 23.78m* **17** MISS WORLD: MISS GRENADA, JENNIFER HOSTE *1970 BBC1 23.76m* **18** MISS WORLD: MISS PERU, MADELINE HARTOG BEL HOUGHTON *1967 BBC1 23.76m* **19** ROYAL VARIETY PERFORMANCE: MICHAEL CRAWFORD *1975 BBC1 22.66m* **20** APOLLO 8 AND 11 SPLASHDOWNS *1968 BBC/ITV 22.54m*

Source: British Film Institute

# CARRY ON FILMS

*'Infamy! Infamy! They've all got it in for me!'*
Kenneth Williams, *Carry On Cleo*

---

### The core of the Carry On cast

Top 5: Kenneth Williams (26 films), Joan Sims (24), Charles Hawtrey (23), Sid James (19), Bernard Bresslaw (18), plus Peter Butterworth, Kenneth Connor, Jim Dale, Jack Douglas, Frankie Howerd, Hattie Jacques, Leslie Phillips, Patsy Rowlands, Terry Scott, Barbara Windsor.

---

Silly caricatures and energetic slapstick, mixed with double entendres, knowing winks and dreadful puns were the main ingredients in the Carry On films: a series of low-budget, farcical flicks churned out at an astonishing rate during the 1960s and 70s, which proved hugely popular with the British public. In total there were 31 Carry On films, as well as various TV specials, which turned their trademark comedic spotlight on everything from camping to Cleopatra. The actors and even the jokes remained consistent from film to film; it was simply the situations that changed. Perceived as following in the British comic tradition of the music hall and seaside postcards, the Carry On formula fell out of favour with the film industry during the 1980s as comedy became harder, more explicit and more socially aware.

## THE FILMS

**1958** *Carry On Sergeant* ❖ **1959** *Carry On Nurse* ❖ **1959** *Carry On Teacher* ❖ **1959** *Carry On Constable* ❖ **1961** *Carry On Regardless* ❖ **1962** *Carry On Cruising* ❖ **1963** *Carry On Cabby* ❖ **1963** *Carry On Jack* ❖ **1964** *Carry On Spying* ❖ **1964** *Carry On Cleo* ❖ **1965** *Carry On Cowboy* ❖ **1966** *Carry On Screaming!* ❖ **1966** *Carry On Don't Lose your Head* ❖ **1967** *Carry On Follow that Camel* ❖ **1967** *Carry On Doctor* ❖ **1968** *Carry On up the Khyber* ❖ **1969** *Carry On Camping* ❖ **1969** *Carry On Again Doctor* ❖ **1970** *Carry On up the Jungle* ❖ **1970** *Carry On Loving* ❖ **1971** *Carry On Henry* ❖ **1971** *Carry On at your Convenience* ❖ **1972** *Carry On Matron* ❖ **1972** *Carry On Abroad* ❖ **1973** *Carry On Girls* ❖ **1974** *Carry On Dick* ❖ **1975** *Carry On Behind* ❖ **1976** *Carry On England* ❖ **1978** *That's Carry On* ❖ **1978** *Carry On Emmanuelle* ❖ **1992** *Carry On Columbus* ❖ **2007** *Carry On London*

# ALFRED HITCHCOCK

The master of suspense is one of the most popular and influential film-makers in the history of cinema. Alfred Hitchcock was also the son of a greengrocer, born in Leytonstone in 1899. It's shocking that he directed more than 50 films in a career that spanned six decades, pioneered various cinematic techniques, had hordes of fans, influenced hundreds of subsequent directors and yet never received an Academy Award for best director.

---

## THE MACGUFFIN

This is an object or plot device around which the plot revolves or which drives the story, but which is otherwise inconsequential. Hitchcock was a huge fan of the MacGuffin, defining the term in a lecture at Columbia University in 1939: *'We have a name in the studio, and we call it the "MacGuffin". It is the mechanical element that usually crops up in any story. In crook stories it is always the necklace and in spy stories it is always the papers.'*

In an interview with François Truffaut in 1966 Hitchcock illustrated the MacGuffin with the following story: *'It might be a Scottish name, taken from a story about two men in a train. One man says, "What's that package up there in the baggage rack?" And the other answers, "Oh that's a MacGuffin". The first one asks, "What's a MacGuffin?" "Well," the other man says, "It's an apparatus for trapping lions in the Scottish Highlands." The first man says, "But there are no lions in the Scottish Highlands," and the other one answers "Well, then that's no MacGuffin!" So you see, a MacGuffin is nothing at all.'*

---

 **The inscription on Hitchcock's tomb reads,** *'I'm in on a plot',* **although allegedly his original suggestion was** *'This is what we do to bad little boys.'*

Hitchcock delivered the shortest acceptance speech in Oscar history: while accepting the Irving Thalberg Memorial Award at the 1967 Oscars, he simply said: *'Thank you.'*

## HITCHCOCKIAN WISDOM

○ *'Television has brought murder back into the home – where it belongs.'*

○ *'To me* Psycho *was a big comedy. Had to be.'*

○ *'There is no terror in the bang, only in the anticipation of it.'*

○ *'The length of a film should be directly related to the endurance of the human bladder.'*

○ *'Always make the audience suffer as much as possible.'*

○ *'When an actor comes to me and wants to discuss his character, I say,* "It's in the script." If he says, "But what's my motivation?" I say, "Your salary."'

○ *'Film your murders like love scenes, and film your love scenes like murders.'*

○ *'If it's a good movie, the sound could go off and the audience would still have a perfectly clear idea of what was going on.'*

○ *'Blondes make the best victims. They're like virgin snow that shows up the footprints.'*

### Cameos

Hitchcock loved to make cameo appearances in his films. In total, he made 37 such appearances if his narration at the start of *The Wrong Man* (1956) is counted. His first appearance was in his third film, *The Lodger* (1926), while his last was in *Family Plot* (1976). A recurring theme in his cameos was for his character to carry a musical instrument.

 Hitchock suffered from ovaphobia, an extreme fear of eggs, and had a morbid fear of the police after being locked in a police cell as a boy on the orders of his father.

# SHERLOCK HOLMES

Sherlock Holmes is Britain's most famous fictional detective. Created by the Scottish author and doctor, Sir Arthur Conan Doyle, he first appeared in a short story in 1887 called 'A Study In Scarlet', before going on to feature in a total of four novels and 56 short stories. Like any self-respecting super-detective, he has a sidekick, Dr John H. Watson. It is Dr Watson who narrates the majority of the Holmes murder mysteries. Although most famous for smoking a pipe, Holmes is more bohemian than a typical British gentleman and isn't averse to occasionally using cocaine and morphine when there are no interesting cases to investigate. *'I abhor the dull routine of existence. I crave for mental exaltation,'* said Holmes of this drug use.

## Some Holmesian wisdom

○ *'There is nothing more deceptive than an obvious fact.'*

○ *'Education never ends, Watson. It is a series of lessons, with the greatest for the last.'*

○ *'When you have eliminated all which is impossible, then whatever remains, however improbable, must be the truth.'*

○ *'I never make exceptions. An exception disproves the rule.'*

 Sherlock Holmes is listed as the *'most portrayed movie character'* in the *Guinness Book of Records* with over 70 actors playing the part in over 200 films.

•

The Sherlock Holmes museum is at 221b Baker Street, the address where Sherlock Holmes lived in the stories.

•

Sir Arthur Conan Doyle once played in goal for Portsmouth FC.

# THE REAL SHERLOCK HOLMES

*'It is certainly to you that I owe Sherlock Holmes and though in the stories I have the advantage of being able to place him in all sorts of dramatic positions I do not think that his analytical work is in the least an exaggeration of some effects which I have seen you produce in the out-patient ward.'*

So wrote Arthur Conan Doyle to Dr Joseph Bell, professor of clinical surgery at Edinburgh University, in 1892. The powers of deduction that Holmes displays are similar to those Bell used to diagnose patients before they said anything about their symptoms or ailments. In appearance Holmes was also similar to Bell, but that is where the similarities end. Bell did not investigate crimes, play the violin or to anyone's knowledge dabble with cocaine and opium.

## NOVELS

*A Study in Scarlet* ♦ *The Sign of the Four* ♦ *The Hound of the Baskervilles* ♦ *The Valley of Fear*

### Sherlock Holmes' verdict on the Ripper

While Sherlock Holmes, sadly, did not exist and so couldn't take on the case (see page 132), his creator Sir Arthur Conan Doyle did, however, construct a theory. He believed that Jack the Ripper was either a woman or disguised himself as a woman to avoid capture and get close to the victims. Advocates of the *'Jill the Ripper'* theory believe that a female murderer either worked or posed as a midwife, which would make it easier to be seen with bloody clothes and not arouse suspicion.

 The image of Sherlock Holmes has appeared on stamps in Britain, Canada, Nicaragua, San Marino and South Africa.

# BRITISH HATS

## THE BOWLER HAT

Manufactured by Thomas and William Bowler, the first bowler hat was designed for the Earl of Leicester in 1850. They rapidly became enormously popular and the traditional headgear of London's city gents. No caricature of an Englishman was complete without one. In Germany, it is known as *melone* and in France as *chapeau melon* due to its melon shape. And, while bowler hats may be as British as you can get, they are also incredibly popular with women in Bolivia.

### FAMOUS BOWLER HAT WEARERS

*Winston Churchill* ■ *Stan Laurel and Oliver Hardy* ■ *Charlie Chaplin* ■ *Benito Mussolini* ■ *Oddjob from James Bond* ■ *Mr Benn the cartoon character* ■ *Steed in* The Avengers *TV series*

## THE POLICE HELMET

The British police helmet is now iconic, but when police first patrolled British streets in 1829, they simply wore tall, reinforced top hats. The design police wear today was based on Prussian military helmets. Although much modified, the basic design remains the same as when the 'new' helmet was issued back in 1865.

## The pork pie hat

Designed in the 19th century, the pork pie hat is like the fedora or trilby, except it has a flat top. Long popular in Britain as everyday headgear, pork pie hats became associated with skinheads and ska fans in the late 1970s .

---

## The flat cap

Although the style can be traced back to the 14th century, flat caps became popular in Britain with working-class men in the 19th century. By the 1920s they were a fashion statement among young men and, by the end of last century, had lost their working-class association and are nowadays worn as everything from casual countrywear to cutting-edge fashion. The Andy Capp comic strip in *The Daily Mirror* still harks back to the cap's roots. Andy, the working-class northern everyman, is never seen without his flat cap.

---

## THE DEERSTALKER

The deerstalker is a hat for hunters, designed to provide protection from the weather and to blend into the background, but its most famous proponent lives in the city and doesn't hunt. Then again, he's also not real. Sherlock Holmes is often pictured wearing a deerstalker, but in Arthur Conan Doyle's books he is not actually described as wearing one. It is in Sidney Paget's accompanying illustrations that he is depicted sporting a deerstalker and this is where the popular image comes from.

---

## The hat tax

Between 1784 and 1811, the British government introduced a tax on men's hats. Each one had to have a revenue stamp attached to its lining, with the cost of the duty dependent on the cost of the hat. While hat tax evasion was punishable by a fine, forgers of hat tax revenue stamps faced the death penalty. The idea was to raise revenue in accordance with the taxpayer's wealth, the logic being that a rich person would have a large collection of pricey hats, while poor people might have the odd cheap hat or none at all.

# JACK THE RIPPER

Just five confirmed kills gives Jack the Ripper a low ranking in the overall league of serial killers, but when it comes to notoriety he inhabits a league of his own. A major part of the public's fascination with Jack the Ripper stems from the fact that he was never caught and more than a century later his true identity is still unknown.

## THE VICTIMS

Although there is considerable debate as to the precise number of people Jack the Ripper killed, the following five are generally accepted to be murders carried out by the same perpetrator. All were women, all worked as prostitutes and all were found in the Whitechapel area:

| Name | Date killed | Victims' aliases |
|------|-------------|------------------|
| MARY ANN NICHOLS | Fri, 31 August, 1888 | *Polly* |
| ANNIE CHAPMAN | Sat, 8 September, 1888 | *Dark Annie* |
| ELIZABETH STRIDE | Sun, 30 September, 1888 | *Long Liz* |
| CATHERINE EDDOWES | Sun, 30 September, 1888 | *Kate Conway, Mary Ann Kelly* |
| Mary Jane Kelly | Fri, 9 November, 1888 | *Marie Jeanette Kelly, Ginger* |

### Mutilations

Except for Stride (whose attack may have been interrupted), mutilations became more severe as the murders went on. Nichols and Stride had all their organs, but Chapman's uterus was taken, and Eddowes had her uterus and a kidney carried away and was left with facial mutilations. While only Kelly's heart was missing from the scene, many of her internal organs were removed and left in her room. Most experts point to throat slashes, mutilations to the victim's abdomen and genital area, removal of internal organs and facial mutilations as the distinctive features of Jack the Ripper.

---

## The FBI psychological profile of Jack the Ripper

• He would have been a white male, aged 28 to 36, living or working in the Whitechapel area.

• In childhood, there was an absent or passive father figure.

• The killer probably had a profession in which he could legally experience his destructive tendencies.

• Jack the Ripper probably ceased his killing because he was either arrested for some other crime, or felt himself close to being discovered as the killer.

• The killer probably had some sort of physical defect which was the source of a great deal of frustration or anger.

Source: www.casebook.org

---

## FAMOUS SUSPECTS

Since the killings numerous well-known people have been put forward as suspects. Here's a selection:

☐ PRINCE ALBERT VICTOR, DUKE OF CLARENCE, known as *'Prince Eddy'*: royal conspiracy theories suggest the murders were committed to cover up a royal indiscretion which had left an illegitimate Catholic heir to the throne. A popular theory in fiction, it is very unlikely he had anything to do with the murders.

☐ LEWIS CARROLL The only link between the author of *Alice in Wonderland* and the murders is in Richard Wallace's 1995 book, *Jack the Ripper, Light-Hearted Friend*, where Wallace argues that certain passages of Carroll's works are anagrams of detailed descriptions of the murders. Critics have shown that similar anagrams can be drawn from other authors' works, including A.A. Milne's *Winnie-the-Pooh*.

☐ WILLIAM WITHEY GULL Queen Victoria's physician has become a popular candidate in novels and movies.

☐ WALTER SICKERT First mentioned as a suspect in one of the royal conspiracy theories , the German-born artist was most likely in France at the time of most of the murders.

# BRITISH KILLERS

## ☠ ANGEL OF DEATH

**Beverly Allitt** killed four children and injured nine others in a 58-day period in 1991, while working as a nurse on the children's ward at Grantham and Kesteven Hospital in Lincolnshire. She suffers from Munchausen's Syndrome by Proxy, which manifests itself in a desire to kill or injure to get attention. She received 13 life sentences in 1993 and relatives of her victims threatened to kill her if she was ever released. Nicknamed the *'Angel of Death'* and *'Killer Nurse'*, it is not known if she murdered any other patients prior to her killing spree in 1991.

## ☠ THE MOORS MURDERERS

Between 1963 and 1965 **Ian Brady** and **Myra Hindley** sexually molested and then murdered five children. They were known as the *'Moors Murderers'* because they disposed of their victims' bodies on Manchester's Saddleworth Moor. Brady, who was born in Glasgow, was already obsessed with Nazi paraphernalia and sadomasochism when he met Hindley at work in Manchester in 1961. The couple were caught when Brady's brother-in-law went to the police in 1966. The death penalty was abolished just one month after the pair were arrested and both received multiple life sentences in 1966. Hindley died in 2002 at the age of 60, having served 36 years behind bars. At the time of her death she was fighting for her release, claiming she was coerced and blackmailed into the killings by Brady. He is in a mental hospital and is unlikely to ever be released.

## ☠ THE STOCKWELL STRANGLER

At 24 **Kenneth Erskine** had the mental age of a 12-year-old and was a violent and dangerous man. All of his victims were pensioners living in the Stockwell area of south London.

---

In 1996 Kenneth Erskine, the *'Stockwell Strangler'*, stopped the attempted murder of Peter Sutcliffe, the *'Yorkshire Ripper'*, by raising the alarm as an inmate tried to strangle Sutcliffe with a pair of stereo headphones.

He broke into their homes and sexually abused and strangled them. Charged with seven murders (although police believe he was responsible for at least another four), he was jailed for a minimum of 40 years in 1988 and will come up for parole in 2028.

## ♝ THE ACID BATH VAMPIRE

**John Haigh** claimed to have drunk the blood of his six victims whom he shot and then disposed of in vats of acid during the 1940s. A convicted forger and fraudster, he was caught after police searched his workshop and found three human gallstones and a pair of false teeth. Sentenced to death he was hanged on August 10, 1949. Haigh claimed to have killed an additional three people, before disposing of their corpses in acid.

## ♝ THE GAY SLAYER

Some people give up smoking or drinking, others vow to find a new job, but **Colin Ireland**'s New Year's resolution in 1993 at the age of 39 was to become a serial killer. He targeted gay men and picked up all five of his victims at the same west London pub, the Coleherne, before strangling them. A former soldier, he had read that to qualify as a serial killer you had to kill five people. He was jailed for life when caught in the same year he made his resolution. It is rumoured that Ireland killed again in prison, strangling a convicted child killer in Wakefield prison.

## ♝ DR DEATH

**Dr Harold Shipman** was Britain's most prolific serial killer, murdering somewhere between 215 and 260 people in West Yorkshire over a 23-year period. He tended to prey on older women (his youngest victim was 41) who were his patients. He was convicted of 15 murders and sentenced to 15 consecutive life sentences in 2000, but hanged himself in prison four years later. Shipman maintained he was innocent up until his death and without a confession it has been difficult to decipher Shipman's motive or the extent of his killings.

## ♝ DENNIS NILSEN

Blocked drains and a bad smell led to **Dennis Nilsen**'s capture. Drains inspectors alerted the police after finding flesh of some sort in Nilsen's drains, having been called in by his neighbours to locate the cause of the unpleasant smell in the street. When the police called on Nilsen, he calmly admitted to murder and pointed the police to human remains in two black bags in his wardrobe. All in all Nilsen is thought to have murdered 15 people. They were all homeless men or male students he picked up and brought back to his flat. He was convicted of six murders and two attempted murders in 1983 and sentenced to life imprisonment.

## ☠ THE YORKSHIRE RIPPER

The so-called Yorkshire Ripper was the subject of one of Britain's biggest ever manhunts, inspiring a wave of terror among women in the north of England during the 1970s. When **Peter Sutcliffe** finally confessed in 1981 he was convicted of the murders of 13 women and attacks on seven others between 1975 and 1980. Many of the women were prostitutes. Sutcliffe claimed to frequently speak with God and said it was a higher power that ordered him to kill the women. It is thought that Sutcliffe attacked and possibly murdered other women in France and Sweden while travelling abroad during the same period. Imprisoned for a minimum of 30 years, he doesn't get on with his peers. In 1996 another prisoner attempted to

strangle Sutcliffe with the wire from a pair of headphones, while the following year Sutcliffe was stabbed in both eyes by a fellow inmate in Broadmoor Hospital. In 2011 he could be released on parole if he is judged no longer to be a danger to the public.

## ☠ THE WESTS

25 Cromwell Street is an address with chilling connotations. It is here that **Fred and Rosemary West** sexually abused, tortured, murdered and buried the majority of their victims. In total, it is believed they killed at least 12 young women in Gloucester. Rosemary West was found guilty of 10 murders in 1995 and sentenced to life imprisonment, while her husband, Fred, committed suicide before his trial. The crimes for which Rosemary was convicted occurred between 1973 and 1979, although the body of her eldest daughter, Heather, was also found at Cromwell Street. She was murdered in 1987 and the police believe it highly unlikely the Wests committed no other killings between 1979 and 1987. In 2001, a documentary-maker claimed Fred West had killed an additional 20 people, but Gloucester police say there is not enough evidence to investigate the claims.

☠ THE DEATH OF CAPTAIN KIDD
When **Captain William Kid** was executed on May 23 1701, it did not run smoothly by any means. For a start, he was drunk, the public executioner was drunk and so was a large proportion of the crowd. Unsurprisingly, amid all the drunkenness, the first attempt didn't work and the rope broke, so he was actually hanged twice even if he didn't feel a thing. Afterwards his body was left to hang in an iron cage over the River Thames, London, for two years as a deterrent to future would-be pirates.

---

### Last man hanging

No single person can lay posthumous claim to be the last to be hanged in Britain as the final two executions took place at the same time, but in different prisons. On 13 August 1964, Peter Anthony Allen (in Walton Prison, Liverpool) and Gwynne Owen Evans (in Strangeways Prison, Manchester) were hanged at the same time. Their crime was the murder of 53-year-old laundry van driver John Alan West, who was killed during a theft. The last woman to be hanged in Britain was Ruth Ellis on 13 July 1955 at London's Holloway Prison for shooting her lover, David Blakely.

---

## THE HANGMAN

Britain's most prolific hangman in the 20th century was Albert Pierrepoint, credited with executing around 450 people. Later in life he became an opponent of capital punishment. One execution that particularly affected him was that of James Corbitt in 1950. Corbitt was a regular in the pub Pierrepoint ran and on the night Corbitt murdered his girlfriend, the murderer and executioner had sung a duet in the pub. Pierrepoint later wrote: *'Executions solve nothing, and are only an antiquated relic of a primitive desire for revenge which takes the easy way and hands over the responsibility for revenge to other people.'*

# SELECTED BRITISH RIOTS

♦ **1355** – ST SCHOLASTICA RIOT, OXFORD, ENGLAND

Proving that acrimony between town and gown has deep roots, a dispute over the quality of wine in The Swindlestock Tavern between locals and university students back in 1355 escalated into armed clashes that left nearly 100 dead.

♦ **1381** – THE PEASANT'S REVOLT, SOUTHERN ENGLAND

Not so much a riot as a mini-revolution in which armed rebels from Kent and Essex led by Wat Tyler marched on London and attempted to storm the Tower of London in protest against a medieval poll tax. It was eventually put down by King Richard.

♦ **1517** – EVIL MAY DAY, LONDON

Britain's first recorded race riot was sparked by a xenophobic speech given by Dr Bell two weeks before May Day in which the preacher encouraged Englishmen to take up arms against immigrants. On May Day itself, a mob of 300 was arrested. No one died during the riot, but 13 of the rioters, including the mob's leader, John Lincoln, were subsequently executed.

♦ **1739** – PORTEOUS RIOTS, EDINBURGH

The Porteous riots were provoked by hatred for one man, Captain John Porteous. This came to a head when an anti-Porteous mob gathered at the hanging of a convicted smuggler. Porteous ordered his troops to fire into the rioting mob, killing six people. The captain was subsequently charged with murder and sentenced to death, but before his punishment could be carried out, a mob broke into the prison where he was held, dragged him out of his cell and lynched him. Passers-by still spit on the spot where a memorial plaque marks Tolbooth prison where Captain Porteous was kept.

♦ **1936** – CABLE STREET RIOT, LONDON

When Oswald Moseley organized a march of the British Union of Fascists through the East End, running battles ensued between anti-fascists and Moseley's 'Blackshirts'. Subsequently, when the Public Order Act 1936 came in, it banned the wearing of political uniforms in public which helped lead to the demise of the 'Blackshirts'.

◆ **1958** – NOTTING HILL RACE RIOTS, LONDON

These race riots started when a group of white youths attacked a Swedish woman, Majbritt Morrison, in west London who was married to a West Indian man. The police intervened, but later that night a mob of Teddy Boys began to attack the homes of black families in the area. The attacks and accompanying riots continued for two weeks as the black community fought back.

◆ **1981** – BRIXTON, LONDON

The Brixton riot occurred against a backdrop of high unemployment, high crime, poor housing, simmering racial tension and deep mistrust of the police. Police were attacked by a crowd after stopping a black youth with a stab wound on Railton Road on the evening of April 10 1981. As more police arrived, more people reacted and soon Railton Road was a full-scale battle zone. Molotov cocktails were thrown for the first time in Britain outside Northern Ireland and nearly 400 people were injured (299 of which were police), while more than 100 vehicles were destroyed.

◆ **1981** – TOXTETH RIOT, LIVERPOOL

In a riot that lasted for nine days, more than 1,000 police were injured, 150 buildings were destroyed and one rioter was killed. Subsequently, the chair of the police authority, Lady Margaret Simey, said that in the face of deep-rooted social issues and institutional police racism the residents of Toxteth would have been 'apathetic fools' if they hadn't reacted.

◆ **1990** – POLL TAX RIOTS, LONDON

What started as a peaceful protest in Trafalgar Square against the Poll Tax descended into violence as the police clashed with the public. The rioters armed themselves with scaffolding poles and other weapons and went on the rampage until about three in the morning. The Poll Tax was abolished and replaced by Council Tax, which isn't much different, but didn't spark a riot.

# LONDON FACT FILE

*'When a man is tired of London, he is tired of life; for there is in London all that life can afford ...'*

Samuel Johnson

---

### London population
**Population:** 7.2 million ❋ **Population density:** 4,573 per square kilometre ❋ **Size:** 1,584 sq km, 609 square miles

---

## LONDON BRIDGES: LENGTHS

WATERLOO BRIDGE 381 m ◇ MILLENNIUM BRIDGE 330 m ◇ HUNGERFORD BRIDGE 320 m ◇ LONDON BRIDGE 300 m ◇ BLACKFRIARS BRIDGE 281 m ◇ TOWER BRIDGE 268 m ◇ HAMMERSMITH BRIDGE 250 m ◇ VAUXHALL BRIDGE 246 m ◇ WESTMINSTER BRIDGE 242 m ◇ LAMBETH BRIDGE 236 m ◇ ALBERT BRIDGE 216 m ◇ BATTERSEA BRIDGE 203 m ◇ SOUTHWARK BRIDGE 203 m ◇ PUTNEY BRIDGE 202 m ◇ CHELSEA BRIDGE 200 m ◇ Wandsworth Bridge 197 m ◇

Source: *Crosstown Traffic* by Chris Roberts

## MISCELLANEOUS LONDON

• London was first settled by the Romans in AD43.

• The first public toilet in London was constructed at The Whittington Longhouse, Bell Wharf Lane, in 1421.

• The first Starbuck's opened in London on the King's Road in Chelsea in 1998.

• London has over 6,000 restaurants.

• In 1971 London Bridge was purchased by an American, and shipped to Lake Havasu City, Arizona, to be displayed as a tourist attraction. Legend has it that the purchaser thought he was actually buying Tower Bridge.

• 30,000 Londoners were killed during World War II by German bombs and rockets.

---

**London is twinned with the following cities:** Berlin, Germany; New York City, USA; Paris, France; Bucharest, Romania; Moscow, Russia; Beijing, China; Tokyo, Japan and Mumbai, India.

---

## LYRICAL LONDON

The capital is a consistant inspiration for songwriters and hundreds of songs name London in their lyrics and titles. Here's a selection:

*'A Bomb in Wardour Street'* by The Jam ◇ *'A Foggy Day in London Town'* by George and Ira Gershwin ◇ *'Blue Piccadilly'* by The Feeling ◇ *'Carnaby Street'* by The Jam ◇ *'Camden Town'* by Suggs ◇ *'Dark Streets of London'* by The Pogues ◇ *'Don't Go Back to Dalston'* by Razorlight ◇ *'Guns of Brixton'* by The Clash ◇ *'I Don't Want to Go to Chelsea'* by Elvis Costello ◇ *'King's Cross'* by the The Pet Shop Boys ◇ *'London Calling'* by The Clash ◇ *'The Only Living Boy in New Cross'* by Carter USM ◇ *'Ska Night Bus to Dalston'* by Bad Manners ◇ *'Waterloo Sunset'* by The Kinks

# EDINBURGH FACT FILE

*'Edinburgh is a mad god's dream.'*
Hugh MacDiarmid, *The Complete Poems*, 1978

✳

*'Edinburgh, in my estimation the most beautiful city in Britain.'*
HRH Prince Charles, *A Vision of Britain*, 1989

✳

*'This profusion of eccentricities, this dream in masonry and living rock is not a drop scene in a theatre, but a city in the world of reality.'*
Robert Louis Stevenson

---

**Population of Edinburgh**
**1755** – 57,195 ✳ **1791** – 81,865 ✳ **1821** – 112,235
✳ **1901** – 316,837 ✳ **1951** – 466,761 ✳ **2005** – 457,830

---

 In the USA the first 20 minutes of *Trainspotting*, a film set in Edinburgh and based on Irvine's Welsh's book, had to be re-dubbed to make the Scottish accents more intelligible.

•

J.K. Rowling, allegedly wrote her first Harry Potter novel in a coffee shop in Edinburgh called Nicolson's Cafe. It is now a Chinese all-you-can-eat restaurant.

---

**Seven writers who lived, worked and/or set their novels in Edinburgh**
*James Boswell ❖ Robert Louis Stevenson ❖ Walter Scott ❖ Ian Rankin ❖ Irvine Welsh ❖ Sir Arthur Conan Doyle ❖ J. K. Rowling*

---

## OTHER NAMES FOR EDINBURGH

| NAME | REASON |
| --- | --- |
| *Athens of the North* | Similar topography to the Greek capital combined with the Scottish Enlightenment in the 18th century. |
| *Auld reekie* | Means *'Old Smoky'* – so named because of the copious amounts of smoke in the air from coal and wood fires and the unpleasant smell derived from unsanitary living conditions. |
| *Britaine's other eye* | Ben Jonson's description in his writing. |
| *Dunedin* | Derives from the Scottish Gaelic, Dùn Èideann. |
| *Edina* | Latin name that appears in the poetry of Robert Burns. |
| *Edinburrie or Embra* | Scots slang for the city. |
| *Empress of the North* | An affectionate nickname from Sir Walter Scott. |

**Edinburgh is twinned with the following cities:** Munich, Germany; Florence, Italy; Nice, France; Vancouver, Canada; Kiev, Ukraine; Aalborg, Denmark; San Diego, USA; Dunedin, New Zealand; Kraków, Poland and Xi'an, China.

## RANGER'S IMPARTIAL LIST OF THE LADIES OF PLEASURE IN EDINBURGH

Published in 1775, this functioned as a sort of guide book to prostitution in the city, containing a comprehensive directory of individual prostitute profiles. Here's an extract:

'Miss DOUGLAS, alias Mrs. RITCHIE, to be found at Mrs YOUNG'S.

ALTHOUGH *we cannot pronounce this Lady as a beauty, yet she is extremely agreeable. She is about 20 years of age, brown hair, good teeth, and very well made. She is good-natured to the highest degree. In a word, those who are fond of the sports of Venus, will find no disagreeable repast; besides, she is emenent in her profession, excessively fond of the service in which she is engaged, has delicate legs and thighs, a soft hand, sparkling eyes, and a heaving breast.'*

# CARDIFF FACT FILE

⇥ *Cardiff was only proclaimed capital city of Wales on 20 December 1955.*

⇥ *Welsh is spoken by 11 per cent of Cardiffians.*

⇥ *Cardiff was once the busiest port in the world.*

---

**Cardiff population**
**1801** – 6,342 ❋ **1851** – 26,630 ❋ **1901** – 172,629
❋ **1951** – 267,356 ❋ **2001** – 305,340
**Population density:** 2.181 per sq km
❋ **Size:** 139.53 sq km

---

## 11 FAMOUS CARDIFFIANS

SHIRLEY BASSEY ❖ CHARLOTTE CHURCH ❖ ROALD DAHL ❖ RYAN GIGGS ❖ COLIN JACKSON ❖ GRIFF RHYS JONES ❖ ROB LACEY ❖ IVOR NOVELLO ❖ SHAKIN' STEVENS ❖ JOHN TOSHACK ❖ CRAIG BELLAMY

---

**Cardiff is twinned with the following cities:** Bergen, Norway; Nantes, France; Stuttgart, Germany and Xiamen, China.

---

## ABOUT CARDIFF

- Cardiff is Europe's youngest capital city after succeeding Swansea in 1955.
- Cardiff City is the only non-English club to have won the FA Cup. They beat Arsenal 2–1 in the 1927 final in what was then known as the 'English Cup'.
- The Romans established a fort at Cardiff in AD75.
- *'Lord Haw Haw'*, real name William Joyce, who made numerous propaganda radio broadcasts for the Nazis during WWII, came from Cardiff. He was hanged in 1946.
- *'Taff'* is slang for a resident of Cardiff or thereabouts. It derives from the River Taff, which runs through the city, and the days when Cardiff was the busiest, and one of the richest, seaports in the world due to coal exports. Originally, the term 'Taff' or 'Taffy' was used for dock workers.

# THE TOWER OF LONDON

Beheadings, torture, celebrity inmates, glittering jewels and exotic animals: built over 1,000 years ago by William the Conqueror, the Tower of London has seen more than its fair share of action. Although most famous as a prison, the Tower has also been a military base, a treasury, an armoury, home to the royal mint and a royal menagerie. Nowadays, it is home to the crown jewels and one of Britain's top tourist attractions.

## EXECUTIONS

Between 1388 and 1747, it's believed that more than 130 people were beheaded at the Tower of London. The first recorded execution at the Tower was of William Hastings for conspiracy against the king in 1483. Six prisoners were privately executed on Tower Green. They were:

*Anne Boleyn (1536) ◇ Margaret Pole, Countess of Salisbury (1541) ◇ Katherine Howard (1542) ◇ Jane Boleyn, Viscountess Rochford (1542) ◇ Lady Jane Grey (1554) ◇ Robert Devereux, 2nd Earl of Essex (1601)*

The last beheading took place in 1747, when Lord Fraser of Lovat was executed after Bonnie Prince Charlie's uprising. The last execution was of a German spy, Josef Jakobs, in 1941. He was shot by firing squad.

### Ghosts

Anne Boleyn, who was beheaded in 1536, is said to walk around with her head under her arm. Sir Walter Raleigh is also said to haunt the Tower. Other ghosts include Guy Fawkes (who was tortured there), Lady Jane Grey (who was beheaded there) and Sir Thomas Beckett. Reportedly, a sentry saw a ghost bear in 1815 and attacked it only to find his bayonet passed straight through it. He died of fright two months later.

## Beefeaters

Dating back to 1485 when they were originally established as King Henry VIII's bodyguard, the sentinels entrusted with guarding the Tower of London probably gained their nickname from the daily ration of meat they received. Others insist it started as an insult, derived from the fact that they were better fed than your average Londoner at the time. The formal title of a Beefeater is *'Yeoman Warder of Her Majesty's Royal Palace and Fortress the Tower of London, and Members of the Sovereign's Body Guard of the Yeoman Guard Extraordinary'*. To qualify as a Yeoman Warder, you need to have retired from the armed forces following at least 22 years of service and possess the Long Service and Good Conduct medals. The first-ever female Beefeater was appointed in January 2007. Beefeaters and their families live in the Tower of London, paying council tax and rent. But, whereas once Beefeaters guarded prisoners with pikes and axes, their main role now is acting as guides to the hordes of tourists that visit.

## THE RAVENS

According to legend, if the ravens leave the Tower of London the monarchy and the tower itself will fall. The myth says that ravens have roosted in the Tower for centuries and that, after the Restoration, mindful of the legend, King Charles II decreed there should always be six ravens resident in the tower. The fact that nowadays they have their wings clipped makes it near impossible for them to escape, but recent research suggests the Tower's ravens can only be traced back to the 19th century when the myth became popular and that, in any case, the Tower has been raven-less for a period since then. During World War II, they apparently died of shock during bombing raids. Needless to say, the Tower didn't fall and after the war replacement ravens were brought in.

# BRITISH BUILDINGS

Durham Cathedral was voted Britain's favourite building in a survey conducted among listeners to Radio 4's *Today* programme in 2001. Cornwall's Eden Project came second, then London's Tate Modern, the National Theatre on London's South Bank and Stansted Airport.

> *'We shape our buildings; thereafter they shape us.'*
> Winston Churchill

---

### Big Ben

Big Ben is the popular name for the Houses of Parliament's clock tower, but it originally referred to the clock's main bell, rather than the building itself. Cast in 1856, the 13-ton bell most likely got its nickname from the chief commissioner of works, Ben Hall, although some suggest it was named after Ben Caunt, a heavyweight prizefighter of the period. The clock, which has four dials, is famed for its reliable timekeeping. When a bomb destroyed part of the Houses of Parliament in 1941, the clock tower remained intact and Big Ben kept ticking. On New Year's Eve 1962, amid heavy snow, however, it slowed down and welcomed the New Year in 10 minutes late. Fifteen years later on 5 August 1976, its chiming mechanism broke down due to metal fatigue and it didn't start again until 9 May 1977. The tower itself, which is not open to the public, is about 316 feet high and has a slight north-west lean of 22 cm due to ground conditions. It also contains cells where Members of Parliament can be imprisoned for breaches of parliamentary privilege, although the last time this happened was in 1880.

---

*'A monstrous carbuncle on the face of a much-loved and elegant friend.'*
Prince Charles' reaction to the proposed extension to the National Gallery, May 1984

## The Iron Bridge

A 100-foot-wide metal bridge spanning part of the River Severn in Shropshire may not sound like much, but at the time it was built, in 1779, it was big news. Bridges back then were made of wood and stone not iron. Abraham Darby had the idea of using iron as a load-bearing material and ultimately his brainchild was an enormous success. Visitors came from all over Europe and the US to see the bridge in action and it was this structure that ushered in iron as the favourite architectural material of the Industrial Revolution. An English Heritage site since 1975, it was also awarded UNESCO World Heritage status in 1986.

## FIVE THINGS YOU MAY NOT KNOW ABOUT HADRIAN'S WALL

Extending across the top of England like a giant scarf is Hadrian's Wall. Constructed in AD122 by the Emperor Hadrian, it took six years to build and extends for 73 miles. It was built in an attempt to prevent raids by tribes in what is now Scotland.

• English Heritage describes Hadrian's Wall as *'the most important monument built by the Romans in Britain'*. It is 80 Roman miles long, which is 73.5 modern miles or 117 kilometres.

• Although many people do so, it is actually forbidden to walk on Hadrian's Wall.

• Hadrian's Wall has featured in both *Robin Hood: Prince of Thieves* (1991) and *King Arthur* (2004).

• Although people generally talk about being *'north of the wall'* as being in Scotland, 90 per cent of Northumberland is north of Hadrian's Wall.

• Britain represented the most northern territory in the Roman Empire and Hadrian's Wall was effectively the northernmost boundary of the empire.

## YORK MINSTER

Building work on what is now the largest medieval
cathedral in England started in 1220, but a church has
existed on the site where York Minster now stands since
AD697. Along with a 10.8-tonne bell called Great Peter, it
possesses the largest medieval stained glass window in
the world in the form of the 76-foot-high Great East
Window. It also has the largest library of any English cathedral, boasting
around 120,000 books and pamphlets. York Minster has its own police
force, responsible for policing the cathedral and the surrounding area.
Some claim that no current police force in the world dates back as far.

 **Prayers can be submitted to the York Minster
prayer box via email.**

### Angel of the North

Before 1998, Tyneside wasn't famous for much apart from being
home to Newcastle United football club. Then Gateshead Council
erected a 20-metre-high, 200-tonne steel sculpture and suddenly it
boasted one of the most famous landmarks in the north of England,
which can be seen for miles around. Created by Turner prize-winning
artist Antony Gormley, the 'Angel of the North' as it is known cost
£800,000 to construct and is Britain's biggest sculpture, boasting a
54-metre wingspan, which is larger than a Boeing 757. Its local
nicknames include 'The Gateshead Flasher' and 'Gabriel'.

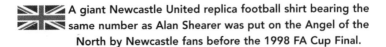 A giant Newcastle United replica football shirt bearing the
same number as Alan Shearer was put on the Angel of the
North by Newcastle fans before the 1998 FA Cup Final.

## Portmeirion

Most famous for providing the location for the 1960s TV series, *The Prisoner*, Portmeirion is a picturesque village in Wales, which actually functions as a large hotel. Visitors don't need to book in, however, but can simply turn up and walk round the grounds. (Accommodation is available in the Hotel Portmeirion, the Castell Deudraeth and 17 self-catering cottages.) Built by architect Clough Williams-Ellis between 1925 and 1975 to show that 'the development of a naturally beautiful site need not lead to its defilement', he was keen to create a Mediterranean-style oasis in northwest Wales. A convention dedicated to *The Prisoner* is held in Portmeirion each year. Other TV shows to have filmed there include *Doctor Who*, *Citizen Smith*, *Brideshead Revisited* and *Bread*.

## STONEHENGE

No one is quite sure why our ancestors lugged those 50-tonne stones all the way from south Wales to the heart of Somerset over 4,000 years ago. It would have taken about 600 people to move one stone half an inch. Stonehenge has been attributed to the Romans, the druids, Merlin the Magician and even the devil, but experts can't even agree on whether it was a religious site, a scientific observatory or both.

## THE GHERKIN

Also known as the Towering Innuendo and the Crystal Phallus, 30 St Mary Axe is better known as The Gherkin. It was designed by architect Sir Norman Foster and built between 2001 and 2004. The building is primarily occupied by a Swiss insurance company, Swiss Re. Despite its curved glass appearance, there is only one piece of curved glass in the whole building, the lens-shaped cap at its summit.

# WESTMINSTER ABBEY

The traditional coronation and burial site for English monarchs, a religious shrine first appeared on the site in AD616 after a fisherman allegedly saw an apparition of St Peter there. A stone abbey was built around 1050 by King Edward the Confessor who decided that he wanted to be buried there, but today's building dates back to the 13th century and the reign of King Henry III. Edward was the first king to be buried there and, except for Henry VIII and Charles I, every monarch up to George II was buried there. Since then, the final resting place of British monarchs has been Windsor Castle.

## FAMOUS BRITISH BURIALS

The bodies of the following famous Brits are all buried at Westminster Abbey:

CLEMENT ATTLEE ◇ CHARLES DARWIN ◇ WILLIAM EWART GLADSTONE ◇ GEORGE FREDERICK HANDEL ◇ DAVID LIVINGSTONE ◇ CHARLES LYELL ◇ THOMAS MACAULAY ◇ SIR ISAAC NEWTON ◇ LAURENCE OLIVIER ◇ WILLIAM PITT, 1ST EARL OF CHATHAM ◇ WILLIAM PITT THE YOUNGER ◇ HENRY PURCELL ◇ ROBERT STEPHENSON ◇ GEORGE VILLIERS

---

### The Unknown Warrior

The tomb of The Unknown Warrior in Westminster Abbey serves as a symbol of all the unidentified British soldiers that have died. It contains the body of an anonymous British soldier killed on an unnamed European battlefield during World War I and buried on November 11, 1920. An army chaplain, Reverend David Railton, allegedly came up with the idea while serving on the Western Front. In 1933, according to a contemporary report in *Time* magazine, Nazi ideologist Alfred Rosenberg laid a wreath bearing a swastika on the tomb. A British war veteran later threw this into the River Thames. The tombstone is the only one in Westminster Abbey on which it is forbidden to walk.

'*Robbing Peter to pay Paul*'. The phrase comes from the fact that once upon a time some of the land belonging to Westminster Abbey, which is dedicated to St Peter, was sold to raise money to repair St Paul's cathedral.

## POETS' CORNER

When Geoffrey Chaucer died on 25 October 1400 he was buried in Westminster Abbey since his house was nearby and he had enjoyed royal favour due to the jobs and positions he had held during his lifetime. In 1556, another poet, Nicholas Brigham erected a more ornate marble monument to mark his tomb. When the Elizabethan poet, Edmund Spenser, was buried near to this tomb in 1599, the idea of a 'Poet's Corner' in the Abbey was born. Since then various poets, playwrights and writers have been buried in this area of the Abbey. Here's a selection:

ROBERT BROWNING ◇ THOMAS CAMPBELL ◇ GEOFFREY CHAUCER ◇ WILLIAM CONGREVE ◇ ABRAHAM COWLEY ◇ WILLIAM DAVENANT ◇ CHARLES DICKENS ◇ JOHN DRYDEN ◇ JOHN GAY ◇ THOMAS HARDY ◇ DR SAMUEL JOHNSON ◇ RUDYARD KIPLING ◇ JOHN MASEFIELD ◇ EDMUND SPENSER ◇ ALFRED TENNYSON

## THOMAS PARR

Born in 1483, Old Parr or Old Tom Parr, as he was known, supposedly lived for 152 years, before being buried in Westminster Abbey. Although he reportedly had an affair and illegitimate child at, even for him, the relatively old age of 100, he put his long life down to a vegetarian diet and adherence to a moral life. Taking his first wife at 80, he married again at the age of 122 and was something of a national celebrity of his day.

# PATRON SAINTS

## ST GEORGE: *National day:* **23rd April**

St George hasn't always been the patron saint of England. In the Middle Ages England had two different patron saints: St Edmund the Martyr and St Edward the Confessor. St George's association with England began in the late 13th century when King Edward I displayed the St George's Cross on his royal banners, alongside the arms of Saints Edmund and Edward. Subsequent kings continued to revere St George and, after the victorious battle at Agincourt, King Henry V marched through a triumphal arch in London topped with a statue of St George in armour. By this time St George had been adopted as the popular patron saint of England.

The real St George was not an Englishman, but a Christian soldier in the Roman army who was martyred in what was Palestine, and what is now Turkey, in the early fourth century. The St George's Cross is thought

to derive from the red cross emblem worn by the crusading order of the Knights Templar. The story of St George and the dragon was a particularly popular one in England by the 15th century and from this sprang the legend of Dragon Hill, which sits on the lower slopes of White Horse Hill in Uffington. It is said this is the site where the dragon was slain by St George and that where the blood gushed out on to the hilltop the grass has forever after refused to grow.

St George is also the patron saint of Canada, Catalonia, Ethiopia, Georgia, Greece, Montenegro, Portugal, Serbia, as well as the cities of Istanbul, Ljubljana and Moscow.

St Andrew is also the patron saint of mariners, fishermen, fishmongers, rope-makers, singers and performers.

## ST ANDREW: *National day:* 30th November

St Andrew was adopted as the patron saint of Scotland in the 10th century. However, he was revered in Scotland before this. The legend goes that in the late 8th century during a battle with the English the Scottish king saw a cloud shaped like a saltire and decided Saint Andrew was watching over them. The king declared that, if they won, then Andrew would be adopted as patron saint. Other legends suggest that relics of St Andrew were brought to Scotland from Constantinople in the 8th century. Little is known about the real St Andrew. He could have been a fisherman in Galilee, later one of Jesus' apostles. Legend says he was crucified by Romans in southern Greece and the diagonal shape of the cross is said to be where the diagonal cross of St Andrew, or saltire, originates from.

## ST DAVID: *National day:* 1st March

St David is unique among patron saints in Britain in that he actually came from the country of which he is patron saint. He was born between 462 and 512 in Pembrokeshire, probably of royal lineage. He founded many monasteries and churches in Wales and England at a time when many Brits were still pagan. Legend has it that, while preaching at the Synod of Llanddewi Brefi, people at the back complained they could neither see nor hear him. The ground on which he stood is then supposed to have risen so everyone could see him. Reportedly over 100 when he died, he was buried where the Cathedral of St David now stands.

 St David is supposed to have been a vegetarian and preached the value of a simple, ascetic life.

# NATIONAL SONGS

## GOD SAVE THE QUEEN

*God save our gracious Queen,*
*Long live our noble Queen,*
*God save the Queen!*
*Send her victorious,*
*Happy and Glorious,*
*Long to reign over us;*
*God save the Queen!*

No one knows who actually composed *'God Save the Queen'*. Similarities have been drawn between pieces of music written by John Bull and Henry Purcell in the 17th century, the French believe the tune was written by Jean-Baptiste Lully, while others cite Thomas Arne, the author of *'Rule Britannia'*, but it's all conjecture. Nobody knows, although the words are often attributed to Henry Carey. Its first public airing is thought to have been in London in 1745 after a performance of Ben Jonson's play, *The Alchemist*, at the Theatre Royal. Although adopted as such from the 18th century onwards, no Royal Proclamation or Act of Parliament has actually ever designated *'God Save the Queen'* as the British national anthem.

---

## THE LOST VERSE

*Lord, grant that Marshal Wade,*
*May by thy mighty aid,*
*Victory bring.*
*May he sedition hush and like a*
*torrent rush,*
*Rebellious Scots to crush,*
*God save the King.*

When the song was first sung in London in 1745 it included the anti-Scottish verse on the left, as the Jacobites, under Bonnie Prince Charlie, had just invaded England in an attempt to restore the Scottish House of Stuart to the throne. For obvious reasons, the verse was omitted when it was adopted as the British national anthem.

## The Sex Pistols

The punk group's second single was ironically named 'God Save the Queen'. It reached number two in the charts, but was banned by the BBC. Here're some of the lyrics:

*God save the queen*
*The fascist regime*
*They made you a moron*
*Potential H-bomb*

*God save the queen*
*She ain't no human being*
*There is no future*
*In England's dreaming*

*Don't be told what you want*
*Don't be told what you need*
*There's no future, no future,*
*No future for you*

## JERUSALEM

Written during the Napoleonic Wars, 'Jerusalem' is a poem by William Blake that was set to music by Hubert Parry in 1916. Sung at Church of England services, by drunken rugby crowds, at Labour Party conferences, by England's cricketers and by the audience in the Royal Albert Hall at the Last Night of the Proms, it's an anthem that seems to transcend cultural boundaries.

The following have all produced modern versions of 'Jerusalem' (The Fat Les electro-dance version was used as the England football team's theme tune at Euro 2000):

**Emerson, Lake and Palmer** ❖ **The Fall** ❖ **Billy Bragg** ❖ **Bruce Dickinson** ❖ **The KLF** ❖ **Fat Les** ❖ **Charlotte Church**

 Thomas Arne set the words of Scottish poet James Thomson's poem, 'Rule Britannia', to music in 1740 and it is this that became the popular patriotic anthem that is sung in Britain today.

 One of England's back-up anthems, used at certain sporting events where England competes separately to the other British nations such as the Commonwealth Games, the tune of 'Land of Hope and Glory' comes from the first march in Edward Elgar's *Pomp and Circumstance* series.

## Scottish anthems

Scotland doesn't officially have a separate national anthem to 'God Save the Queen', but when it participates in sporting events either 'Flower Of Scotland' or 'Scotland the Brave' tend to be played. Interestingly, 'Flower of Scotland', which was written by folk musician Roy Williamson in 1966 is impossible to play properly on the bagpipes as one of the notes in the song is not available to play on the instrument.

## WELSH NATIONAL ANTHEM

'Hen Wlad Fy Nhadau' (Land Of My Fathers) is not officially or legally a national anthem; tradition means it is the national anthem for Wales. It is always sung in Welsh, but here's the English translation of the first verse:

*This land of my fathers is dear to me*
*Land of poets and singers, and people of stature*
*Her brave warriors, fine patriots*
*Shed their blood for freedom*

# MUSIC

## ORIGINAL GLASTONBURY FESTIVAL LINE-UP 1970

*The Kinks ◇Steamhammer ◇Duster Bennet ◇Alan Bown ◇Wayne Fontana ◇Stackridge ◇Amazing Blondel ◇Ian Anderson ◇Ian Hunt ◇ Marsupilami ◇Originn ◇Mad Mick ◇Derek James ◇Marc Bolan ◇Keith Christmas ◇Al Stewart ◇Quintessence ◇Sam Apple Pie ◇Roy Harper*

On 19 September 1970, the day after Jimi Hendrix died, between 1,000 and 2,500 paid just £1 to enjoy the above line-up at the original Glastonbury Festival. Milk from the farm was free for festival-goers.

## SOME POP STARS' REAL NAMES

STEVE STRANGE - *Steve Harrington* ❖ ELTON JOHN – *Reg Dwight* ❖ BOY GEORGE – *George O'Dowd* ❖ DR ROBERT – *Bruce Howard* ❖ CLIFF RICHARD – *Harry Webb* ❖ BUSTER BLOODVESSEL – *Douglas Trendle* ❖ ENYA – *Eithne Nibhraonain* ❖ CHRIS DE BURGH – *Christopher Davidson* ❖ RICHARD CLAYDERMAN – *Philippe Pages* ❖ ADAM ANT – *Stuart Goddard* ❖ DAVID SYLVIAN – *David Batt* ❖ SUGGS (MADNESS) – *Graham McPherson* ❖ FREDDIE MERCURY - *Frederick Bulsara/Farok Bulsara* ❖ JENNIFER RUSH – *Heidi Stern* ❖ ELVIS COSTELLO – *Declan Patrick MacManus* ❖ GEORGE MICHAEL – *Georgios Panayiotou* ❖ STING – *Gordon Sumner* ❖ BONO – *Paul David Hewson* ❖ RINGO STARR – *Richard Starkey*

## Early names of some famous bands
Bangles – *Bangs* ❊ Beatles – *Carl and the Passions* ❊ Black Sabbath – *Polka Tulk* ❊ Depeche Mode – *Composition of Sound*

## Banned in Britain

You can tell a lot about a country by the things they ban. The following records were banned by the BBC when they first came out.

**Jane Birkin** *'Je T'aime'* 1969 ○ **Frankie goes to Hollywood** *'Relax'* 1983 ○ **The Au Pairs** *'Come Again* 1981 ○ **Lil Louis** *'French Kiss'* 1989 ○ **Ivor Biggun** *'The Winkers Song (misprint)'* 1978 ○ **Troggs** *'I Can't Control Myself'* 1966 ○ **Rolling Stones** *'Let's Spend the Night Together'* 1967 ○ **The Stranglers** *'Peaches'* 1977 ○ **Paul McCartney & Wings** *'Hi Hi Hi '* 1972 ○ **Max Romeo** *'Wet Dream'* 1969 ○ **Donna Summer** *'Love to Love You Baby'* 1976 ○ **Hawkwind** *'Urban Guerrilla'* 1970 ○ **Sex Pistols** *'God Save the Queen'* 1977

Interestingly, The Kinks' *'Lola'* was originally banned by BBC Radio when it came out in 1972 on advertising grounds because it mentioned Coca-Cola, but this was later changed to Cherry Cola to get airplay.

## GOLDEN OLDIES

According to *The Times*, *'a lyrical homage to the English countryside written in the shadow of World War One'* is Britain's favourite piece of classical music. Vaughan Williams' *'The Lark Ascending'* came top in a Classic FM poll of 2007.

## LAST NIGHT OF THE PROMS

The Last Night of the Proms is an indulgent celebration of *'Britishness'*. *'Proms'* is short for *'Promenades'* and Prommers have no seats, but are free to stroll near the Albert Hall stage. This is as near as classical music gets to a *'moshpit'*. In fancy dress and armed with flags and horns, Prommers bob up and down to such patriotic staples as *'Jerusalem'*, *'Land of Hope and Glory'* and *'Fantasia on British Sea Songs'*.

# THE BEATLES

## Beatles albums

*Please Please Me* **(1963)** ❊ *With The Beatles* **(1963)** ❊ *A Hard Day's Night* **(1964)** ❊ *Beatles For Sale* **(1964)** ❊ *Help!* **(1965)** ❊ *Rubber Soul* **(1965)** ❊ *Revolver* **(1966)** ❊ *Sgt. Pepper's Lonely Hearts Club Band* **(1967)** ❊ *Magical Mystery Tour* **(1967)** ❊ *White Album* **(1968)** ❊ *Yellow Submarine* **(1969)** ❊ *Abbey Road* **(1969)** ❊ *Let It Be* **(1970)** ❊ *1962–1966* **(1973)** ❊ *1967–1970* **(1973)** ❊ *Live At The BBC* **(1994)** ❊ *Anthology 1* **(1995)** ❊ *Anthology 2* **(1996)** ❊ *Anthology 3* **(1996)** ❊ *Yellow Submarine Songtrack* **(1999)** ❊ *1* **(2000)** ❊ *Let It Be... Naked* **(2003)**

### UK NUMBER ONE HITS

| Song | Date | Weeks at Number 1 | Song | Date | Weeks at Number 1 |
|---|---|---|---|---|---|
| 'From Me To You' | 2 May 1963 | 7 | 'Paperback Writer' | 23 June 1966 | 2 |
| 'She Loves You' | 12 Sept 1963 | 6 | 'Eleanor Rigby/Yellow Submarine' | 18 Aug 1966 | 4 |
| 'I Want To Hold Your Hand'* | 12 Dec 1963 | 5 | 'All You Need Is Love' | 19 July 1967 | 3 |
| 'Can't Buy Me Love' | 2 April 1964 | 3 | 'Hello Goodbye'* | 6 Dec 1967 | 7 |
| 'A Hard Day's Night' | 23 July 1964 | 3 | 'Lady Madonna' | 27 Mar 1968 | 2 |
| 'I Feel Fine'* | 10 Dec 1964 | 5 | 'Hey Jude' | 11 Sept 1968 | 2 |
| 'Ticket To Ride' | 22 April 1965 | 3 | 'Get Back' | 23 April 1969 | 6 |
| 'Help!' | 5 Aug 1965 | 3 | 'Ballad Of John And Yoko' | 11 June 1969 | 3 |
| 'Day Tripper/We Can Work It Out'* | 16 Dec 1965 | 5 | *Christmas number 1 | | |

Cher's first solo recording was the novelty single *Ringo, I Love You.*

## SGT. PEPPER COVER

Designed by Peter Blake and photographed by Michael Cooper, the Sgt. Pepper album cover is probably one of the most famous pieces of cover artwork of all time. Here are some of the people whose images appeared on the album:

*Edgar Allen Poe ◆ Fred Astaire ◆ George Bernard Shaw ◆ Marlon Brando ◆ Lenny Bruce ◆ William Burroughs ◆ Lewis Carroll ◆ Aleister Crowley ◆ Tony Curtis ◆ Marlene Dietrich ◆ Diana Dors ◆ Bob Dylan ◆ Albert Einstein ◆ W.C. Fields ◆ Carl Gustav Jung ◆ Oliver Hardy ◆ Aldous Huxley ◆ Stan Laurel ◆ Sonny Liston ◆ Dr. David Livingstone ◆ Karl Marx ◆ Richard Merkin ◆ Marilyn Monroe ◆ Sir Robert Peel ◆ Terry Southern ◆ Albert Stubbins ◆ Stuart Sutcliffe ◆ Shirley Temple ◆ Dylan Thomas ◆ H.G. Wells ◆ Mae West ◆ Oscar Wilde.*

## BEATLES BACK ROLF

The Beatles sang backing vocals on Rolf Harris's *Tie Me Kangaroo Down, Sport* when he sang it on a BBC radio show in 1963. Harris completely customized the original lyrics to a version that was especially written for the Beatles:

*'Cut yer hair once a year boys
Don't ill-treat me pet dingo, Ringo
George's guitar is on the blink, I think
Prop me up by the wall, Paul
Keep the hits coming on, John.'*

While watching a Beatles-related webcam which focused on Mathew Street, Liverpool where the Cavern Club is located, a Beatles fan in the US saw burglars breaking into a sports shop and called the Merseyside police, who arrested the three men.

## The fifth Beatle

Over the years various people have laid claim to being the fifth Beatle. Here are a few examples:

**Stuart Sutcliffe** *Credentials:* Original bass player, sometimes credited with coining the band's name. Died at 21 of a cerebral haemorrhage, having already left the Beatles.

**Billy Preston** *Credentials:* Played on the 1970 *Let It Be* album and on the 'I Want You (She's So Heavy)' and 'Something', on *Abbey Road* (1969). Lennon wanted him in the band, McCartney didn't.

**Pete Best** *Credentials:* Original drummer who was fired from the band in 1962, before they took off.

**George Martin** *Credentials:* Producer on almost all of the Beatles' albums and credited by some with creating the band's sound.

**Brian Epstein** *Credentials:* Original manager from 1961 until his death in 1967, who helped the Beatles make their initial mark on the musical map. 'He's the fifth Beatle, if there ever was one,' said George Martin in the 1990s.

**Tony Sheridan** *Credentials:* Recorded an album with the Beatles, which was released in 1962 in Germany under the banner 'Tony Sheridan and The Beat Brothers' as the word 'Beatles' was thought to sound too like the German, *pidels*, slang for penises.

**Neil Aspinall** *Credentials:* Assistant, road manager and close personal friend to the band.

**Alf Bicknell** *Credentials:* Driver, roadie and friend to the Beatles.

**Mal Evans** *Credentials:* Roadie who played Hammond organ on 'You Won't See Me' and a solo on an alarm clock on 'A Day in the Life'.

**George Best** *Credentials:* He was a celebrity, good-looking and lived the lifestyle of a rock star. After scoring two goals for Manchester United in a 5–1 win against Benfica, the Portuguese press dubbed him 'El Beatle'.

**Murray the K** *Credentials:* A New York DJ referred to as the 'fifth Beatle' by George Harrison.

**Charles Manson** *Credentials:* Mass murderer Manson interpreted a chapter in the Book of Revelation as meaning he was the fifth Beatle.

# SPORTS BRITAIN GAVE THE WORLD

*'I tend to think that cricket is the greatest thing that
God ever created on earth – certainly greater than sex,
although sex isn't too bad either.'*
Harold Pinter

Everyone knows Britain invented football, rugby and cricket, but the
British have exported various other games around the globe as well.

## ➤ BASEBALL

Americans might like to claim that they devised their national sport, but baseball was invented in England. Some people in the US like to pretend that baseball is a unique, American interpretation of rounders (which was also invented by Brits), but it isn't. Baseball's first mention in Britain was in a book called *A Little Pretty Pocket Book* by John Newbery, published in 1762. Jane Austen also mentions the sport in her book *Northanger Abbey*, which she began writing in 1798. The first game of baseball wasn't played in the US until 1838.

## ➤ SQUASH

Conceived by pupils at Harrow School in England during the 19th century as a derivative of 'rackets', the school installed the first-ever purpose-built squash courts during the 1860s. It's proved a popular export, particularly in Australia, the US and Asia.

## ➤ GOLF

Scotland boasts the oldest golf course in the world in The Old Links at Musselburgh and Scots like to claim that they invented the sport. But so do the Dutch and Chinese. It's open to debate. King James II was supposed to have banned football and 'ye golf' back in 1457 and the argument is that while there were various stick-and-ball games around, using holes rather than targets was a Scottish innovation. The Dutch counter that golf's first mention in the Netherlands was in 1297 and claim the term golf is a bastardization of the Dutch word *kolf*, meaning club or bat. More recently, a Chinese professor claimed to have unearthed evidence in 2006 that proved golf was played in China all the way back in AD945. Those who believe that Scotland is golf's spiritual and cultural home are unimpressed. 'Stick and ball games have been around for many centuries, but golf as we know it today, played over 18 holes, clearly originated in Scotland,' says a spokesman for the Royal and Ancient Golf Club.

## ⤃ BADMINTON

Sports using shuttlecocks and rackets date back to ancient times, but the formal birthplace of the sport that is played today is Badminton House in Gloucestershire, home of the Duke of Beaufort, where guests played the game during the 1860s and 1870s. The first rules of badminton were set out by the Bath Badminton Club in 1877 with the Badminton Association of England publishing the first proper set of rules in 1893.

## ⤃ SNOOKER

It may not have been invented in Britain, but snooker was still the brainchild of a Brit. Legend has it that while posted in Jabalpur in India in 1875 Colonel Sir Neville Francis Fitzgerald Chamberlain came up with a variation on billiards that became snooker. The term 'snooker' was army slang for a first-year cadet and supposedly became associated with the game when Chamberlain suggested there were all 'snookers' at the new game he'd invented.

## ⤃ CROQUET

Nothing is quite as quintessentially British as the garden game of croquet, which is perhaps why nobody else in the world bothers to play it.

---

 In May 2006 pictures of Deputy Prime Minister John Prescott playing croquet at his official residence, Dorneywood, were published in the *Daily Mail* shortly after a sex scandal forced him to resign his ministerial responsibilities while retaining his salary and privileges. Prescott was roundly canned, but Asda reported a 300 per cent increase in sales of croquet sets.

## Boxing

People may have been having punch-ups since we descended from the trees, but boxing as the sport it is today is a British invention. Yes, the ancient Greeks boxed in the Olympics and bare-knuckle fights have always been around, but the rules enforced by today's professional and Olympic boxing bodies are based on the Marquess of Queensbury Rules, devised in 1867. Written by John Chambers and endorsed by the ninth Marquess, they were designed to improve on the London Prize Ring rules and regulate prize fighting as a 'Gentleman's Sport'.

### THE MARQUESS OF QUEENSBURY RULES

❶ To be a fair stand-up boxing match in a 24-foot ring, or as near that size as practicable. ❷ No wrestling or hugging allowed. ❸ The rounds to be of three minutes' duration, and one minute's time between rounds. ❹ If either man falls through weakness or otherwise, he must get up unassisted, 10 seconds to be allowed him to do so, the other man meanwhile to return to his corner, and when the fallen man is on his legs the round is to be resumed and continued until the three minutes have expired. ❺ If one man fails to come to the scratch in the 10 seconds allowed, it shall be in the power of the referee to give his award in favour of the other man. ❻ A man hanging on the ropes in a helpless state, with his toes off the ground, shall be considered down. ❼ No seconds or any other person to be allowed in the ring during the rounds. ❽ Should the contest be stopped by any unavoidable interference, the referee to name the time and place as soon as possible for finishing the contest; so that the match must be won and lost, unless the backers of both men agree to draw the stakes. ❾ The gloves to be fair-sized boxing gloves of the best quality and new. ❿ Should a glove burst, or come off, it must be replaced to the referee's satisfaction. ⓫ A man on one knee is considered down and if struck is entitled to the stakes. ⓬ No shoes or boots with springs allowed. ⓭ The contest in all other respects to be governed by revised rules of the London Prize Ring.

---

## Strawberries and cream

In 2006, 28,000 kilos of strawberries and 7,000 litres of cream were sold at Wimbledon. This wasn't exceptional and similar amounts are sold each year. Mind you, they also sold 22,000 slices of pizza and 23,000 bananas in 2006. King George V is believed to have started the tradition of eating strawberries and cream while watching the action.

---

### ➤➤ WIMBLEDON

While Wimbledon is one of the highlights of the British sporting calendar, it now also functions as a source of annual humiliation. The truth is that Brits are terrible at tennis. Between 1936 and 2006, not a single Brit has won the men's singles title. The women haven't fared much better, with Virginia Wade the last female champion in 1977.

### ➤➤ THE ORIGINS OF RUGBY

The story goes that rugby was born in 1823 when William Webb Ellis picked the ball up during a game of football at Rugby school. It's a myth. It grew out of football when certain parties decided the rules were becoming too soft.

• The first written rules of rugby were published by three Rugby schoolboys in 1845. In 1848, the Old Rugbeians challenged the Old Etonians to a game of football and outrage at the use of hands caused footballing purists to draw up the 'Cambridge Rules', a code of conduct for football. In 1863, the Blackheath Club chose to leave the FA when the latter confirmed bans on 'hacking' and handling. Other rugby teams followed suit and the RFU came into being in 1871.

---

 Wimbledon isn't the tennis tournament's real name. It is actually called 'The Championships'.

•

There have only been five Rugby World Cups with a British side (England) only triumphing once in 2003.

• At first, no points were given for a try: the idea was that you were allowed 'a try' at kicking the ball between the posts. By 1892 the oval was compulsory, an evolutionary leap made possible when inner tubes replaced pig's bladders. Rugby Union remained amateur until 1995 and today's Rugby World Cup is still played for the Webb Ellis trophy despite the fact he didn't actually invent the sport.

## CRICKET

*'Cricket is basically baseball on valium.'*
Robin Williams

### The Ashes

Every two years or so, England play Australia for The Ashes. It's a strange competition, because it takes its name from a newspaper article. When England lost to Australia for the first time at home, the English newspaper, *The Sporting Times*, published a mock obituary to English cricket, concluding that, 'The body will be cremated and the ashes taken to Australia'. When an England team set off to tour Australia a few weeks later, they declared that they were going to return with 'the ashes'. England won two out of three tests and during the tour the England captain, Ivo Bligh, was presented with an urn, intended to represent 'the ashes'. A popular misconception is that the urn contains the ashes of the stumps or a ball used during the test and that this is what the teams compete for when they meet. In fact, the original urn was a personal gift to Bligh and, though Bligh's widow eventually gave the urn to the MCC, it resides in a museum at Lord's and isn't presented to the winner of each Ashes test series. And, although it probably contains the ashes of a cricket bail, this is by no means 100 per cent certain. During England's 2006–7 Ashes tour they travelled with a poet-in-residence, David Fine, who was sponsored by the Arts Council. It did little good: England were hammered 5–0. What cricketing term rhymes with 'whitewash'?

## A country in love with cockfighting

Before it was banned in the mid-18th century, cockfighting was arguably Britain's national sport. Shrove Tuesday in particular was a big day in the cockfighting calendar. Cockpits were made illegal in 1835, but the sport wasn't banned outright in England and Wales until 1849 and not until 1895 in Scotland.

## FOOTBALL

Home to the oldest football competition in the world (the FA Cup) and the oldest football league in the world, Britain is football's spiritual home. And Brits are obsessed with the game. It's natural. After all, to all intents and purposes, Brits invented the modern game.

### Top English Teams

| CLUB | NUMBER OF LEAGUE TITLES (LT) | | FA CUP WINS (FA) | |
|---|---|---|---|---|
| Liverpool | LT:18 FA:7 | Aston Villa | LT:7 | FA:7 |
| Manchester United | LT:16 FA:11 | Sunderland | LT:6 | FA:2 |
| Arsenal | LT:13 FA:10 | Newcastle United | LT:4 | FA:6 |
| Everton | LT:9 FA:5 | Sheffield Wednesday | LT:4 | FA:3 |

**Teams that have been English League Champions three times with FA Cup wins in brackets:** Chelsea (4), Blackburn Rovers (0), Huddersfield Town (1), Wolverhampton Wanderers (4), Leeds United (1).

**Teams that have been English League Champions twice:** Burnley (1), Derby County (1), Manchester City (4), Portsmouth (1), Preston North End (2), Tottenham Hotspur (8).

**Teams that have been English League Champions once:** Ipswich Town (1), Nottingham Forest (2), Sheffield United (4), West Bromwich Albion (5).

Correct as of 2006–07 season

## TOP 5 PREMIERSHIP FOOTBALLERS' CARS IN 2007

**1** BMW X5 £49,980 Owned by 25 footballers, including *John Terry, Wayne Rooney, Cristiano Ronaldo* and *Rio Ferdinand*. **2** RANGE ROVER SPORT £54,500 Owned by 23 players. **3** PORSCHE 911 TURBO £97,840 Owned by 16 players. **4** BENTLEY CONTINENTAL GT £117,500 Owned by 15 players. **5** ASTON MARTIN DB9 £110,000 Owned by 14 players. Source: *Nuts* magazine

## FOOTBALL HOOLIGANISM

Britain has been the source of many cultural exports, but one of the most infamous is football hooliganism. Sometimes termed the 'English disease', football hooliganism dates back almost as far as the invention of football itself. In Britain it started in the late 1800s and by the 1960s was regarded by the police as a serious problem. The police have attempted to squash it, but the phenomenon has never gone away and although fans fight less in stadiums than they used to, rival gangs, known as 'firms' simply arrange to meet for dust-ups away from the stadium. Outside Britain hooliganism is rife across Europe and in Latin America. In these foreign circles British is respected for 'inventing' football hooliganism. In fact, one of the most popular TV personalities in Mexico during World Cups is 'El Hooligan', a comic parody of a British thug.

**Football gangs are known as 'firms'. Here are some of them:**
CARDIFF Soul Crew ◇ CHELSEA Headhunters ◇ DERBY COUNTY Derby Lunatic Fringe ◇ RANGERS Inter City Firm ◇ LEEDS UNITED Service Crew ◇ MILLWALL Bushwackers ◇ PORTSMOUTH 6.57 Crew

> ## Roy of the Rovers
>
> Kidnappings, assassination attempts, a helicopter crash and the saxophone player from Spandau Ballet: forget about the football, it's a wonder Roy of the Rovers, from the comic strip of the same name, ever actually had time to play. Long before the *Footballers' Wives* scriptwriters produced their soccer soap opera, *Roy of the Rovers* realized the value of interweaving football with melodrama. Its plots, if anything, were more outrageous. Melchester Rovers won the 1986 League Cup with a line-up including Bob Wilson, Emlyn Hughes alongside Martin Kemp and Steve Norman from Spandau Ballet.
>
> Although many associate Roy's team with Manchester United, rumour has it that *Tiger* editor Derek Birnage and original scriptwriter, Frank Pepper, actually modelled the Rovers on the Arsenal team of the Fifties. Roy isn't based on anyone real, though that doesn't stop sports writers from describing countless footballers as 'doing a Roy of the Rovers' when they turn in a match-winning performance.

# BIG RON

Ron Atkinson, former television pundit and commentator, speaks football nonsense, or what is known as 'Ronglish':

*'The Spaniards have been reduced to aiming aimless balls into the box.'*

✳

*'If Glenn Hoddle said one word to his team at half-time, it was concentration and focus.'*

✳

*'Well, either side could win it, or it could be a draw.'*

*'They've picked their heads up off the ground and they now have a lot to carry on their shoulders.'*

✳

*'That was Pele's strength – holding people off with his arm.'*

✳

*'He dribbles a lot and the opposition don't like it – you can see it all over their faces.'*

# HORSE RACING

***'Sex is an anti-climax after that!'***
Grand National-winning jockey Mick Fitzgerald

## HORSE RACING FACTS

• In 1750, 'gentlemen' and nobles formed the Jockey Club using the Star & Garter, Pall Mall as their HQ, but soon relocated to Newmarket.
• Today, there are two kinds of horse racing in Britain: flat and jumping. There are 19 flat courses, 24 jumps courses and 17 dual purpose.
• The five classics of the flat racing season are The Stan James 2000 and 1000 Guineas, the Vodafone Oaks, The Vodafone Derby and the Ladbrokes St Leger.
• Racehorse names are limited to 18 letters including spaces.
• Amateur jockeys are identified in the race card by the prefix 'Mr, Mrs, Captain', etc., to indicate their status.

### Racing terms

**Ante-Post:** Betting well in advance of a race – i.e. days, weeks, months ❋ **Calling a cab:** When a rider puts an arm up after a mistake at a fence to keep his balance ❋ **Genuine:** A horse which always does its best ❋ **Hacked Up:** Won a race easily ❋ **Tic-Tac:** Bookmakers' method of conveying information and odds with hand movements

## THE GRAND NATIONAL

The Grand National is a British institution. Everyone from diehard gee-gee followers to grannies 'has a flutter'. First run in 1837, the gruelling steeplechase consists of 40 horses negotiating 40 fences on a four and a half mile course. Red Rum is the only horse to win three times (in 1973, 1974 and 1977). 'Rummy' also came second in 1975 and 1976.

# BIZARRE BETS

Each year William Hill draws up odds for odd events that could occur during the year in Britain. Here's a selection of its offerings for 2007.

**1000/1** Kate Moss to ditch Pete Doherty and become a nun

**1000/1** National Service to be reinstated

**1000/1** London Eye to shut down after being sued for invasion of privacy by nearby residents

**1000/1** Archbishop of Canterbury to confirm the Second Coming.

**1000/1** Arsenal-Spurs to announce official plans to amalgamate as London FC

**500/1** London Congestion Charge to be abolished

**500/1** Conclusive proof that the Loch Ness Monster is alive

**500/1** Buckingham Palace sold off for affordable housing

**200/1** Snow during Wimbledon

**100/1** All-British final at Wimbledon

**100/1** Sharon Osbourne to leave Ozzy Osbourne for Simon Cowell

**100/1** Official confirmation of existence of intelligent extra-terrestrial life

**66/1** Tony Blair to grow a moustache

**50/1** George Michael to marry a female in 2007

**40/1** John Prescott to run off with the other Cheeky Girl

**25/1** Pop star Robbie Williams to marry or come out

**25/1** Big Ben to fail to chime due to adverse weather

**20/1** Kate Moss to marry Pete Doherty and have their first child in 2007

**12/1** Robbie Williams to have laser tattoo removal

**10/1** Beatles to have a No.1 single

**9/1** Madonna and Guy Ritchie to adopt another baby in 2007

**8/1** Robbie Williams to rejoin Take That

**6/1** Posh & Becks to file for divorce

**6/1** Charlotte Church to announce she is pregnant with Gavin Henson's baby

**5/1** Posh & Becks to adopt a child

**5/1** Queen to abdicate

**4/1** The Queen Vic to burn down in *EastEnders*

# BRITISH ART

*'The moment you cheat for the sake of beauty, you know you're an artist.'*
David Hockney

## FAMOUS BRITISH ARTISTS

Although Britain has some of the world's greatest galleries, there were few, if any, great painters before Sir Joshua Reynolds, George Stubbs and Thomas Gainsborough in the 18th century. William Blake, John Constable and J.M.W. Turner, followed, then the Pre-Raphaelites and William Morris. Last century produced Sir Jacob Epstein, Henry Moore, Lucian Freud, Francis Bacon and David Hockney. Of more recent vintage are Damien Hirst, Sarah Lucas and Tracey Emin.

---

### BRITAIN'S FAVOURITE PAINTINGS AS VOTED FOR BY RADIO 4 LISTENERS IN 2005

❶ *The Fighting Temeraire* by J.M.W. TURNER, 1838–39, The National Gallery, London

❷ *The Hay Wain* by JOHN CONSTABLE, 1821, The National Gallery, London

❸ *A Bar at the Folies Bergère* by EDOUARD MANET, 1882, The Courtauld Institute, London

❹ *The Arnolfini Portrait* by JAN VAN EYCK, 1434, The National Gallery, London

❺ *Mr and Mrs Clark and Percy* by DAVID HOCKNEY, 1970, Tate Britain. London

❻ *Sunflowers* by VINCENT VAN GOGH, 1888, The National Gallery, London

❼ *The Reverend Walker Skating on Duddingston Loch* by SIR HENRY RAEBURN, 1784, The National Gallery of Scotland

❽ *The Last of England* by FORD MADDOX BROWN, 1860, Birmingham Museums and Art Gallery, Fitzwilliam Museum, Cambridge

❾ *The Baptism of Christ* by PIERO DELLA FRANCESCA, c. 1450, The National Gallery, London

❿ *The Rake's Progress* by WILLIAM HOGARTH, 1733–34, Sir John Soane's Museum, London

*'Lots of ambitious work by young artists ends up in a dumpster after its warehouse debut. So an unknown artist's big glass vitrine holding a rotting cow's head covered by maggots and swarms of buzzing flies may be pretty unsellable. Until the artist becomes a star. Then he can sell anything he touches.'*

Charles Saatchi

## The Turner Prize

Awarded each year to a British visual artist under the age of 50, the Turner Prize causes an enormous amount of controversy due both to the exhibits and the merits of the winners. The press, therefore, love it. Here are some of the winners:

| YEAR | ARTIST | TITLE OF WORK | DESCRIPTION |
| --- | --- | --- | --- |
| 2005 | SIMON STARLING | *Shedboatshed* | A shed that had been turned into a boat and then into a shed |
| 2004 | JEREMY DELLER | *Memory Bucket* | Documentary about George W. Bush's hometown in Texas and the siege in nearby Waco |
| 2001 | MARTIN CREED | *The Lights Going On and Off* | Installation of lights going on and off |
| 1998 | CHRIS OFILI | *No Woman, No Cry* | Canvas featuring acrylic paint, oil paint, polyester resin, paper collage, map pins and elephant dung |
| 1995 | DAMIEN HIRST | *Mother and Child, Divided* | Sculptures featured among other things a cow in formaldehyde |

 **Even though Tracy Emin's** *My Bed* **(an unmade bed with empty booze bottles, fag butts, stained sheets and worn underwear) gained all the media attention when it was nominated, it never won the Turner Prize.**

# NUDE AND RUDE BRITAIN

*'We are not ashamed to stand up and say we are naturists – it is not perverted, disgusting or ludicrous.'*

British Naturism

## BRITISH NATURISM

Although Brits are notoriously prudish about nudity, not everyone living in Britain is reticent about letting their nether regions enjoy the open air. British Naturism boasts more than 15,000 members and the organization estimates that something like one million people in Britain practise some form of nude sunbathing or social nudity. However, even British Naturism admits: *'Culturally, the British often see the naked form as shameful, offensive, silly or overtly sexual and so if a member of the public comes across a naked person unexpectedly they often complain to authorities.'*

• A quarter of Brits have swum naked. • 88% of Brits believe that naturists are harmless, while 40% believe they are sensible. • 82% of Brits believe nudity should be legal on some beaches. • 14% of Brits sunbathe nude to achieve an all-over tan. • 7% of Brits believe naturism is disgusting. • 2% of Brits believe naturism should be illegal. • 1% of Brits would call the police if they stumbled across a group of nude people.

Source: *'Summary of National Opinion Poll'* commissioned by the British Naturism organization in 2000

---

### The naked rambler

In June 2003 former Royal Marine, Stephen Gough, embarked on the oft-trodden 900-mile trek between Land's End and John O'Groats. The only difference between him and those in whose footsteps he trod is that he wasn't wearing any clothes. Right through the winter, braving freezing temperatures, he wore just socks, walking boots, a hat and his rucksack.

---

### Britain's top nudist beaches

FRAISETHORPE, Bridlington ❋ WILD PEAR BAY, Combe Martin ❋ VAULT BEACH, Gorran Haven ❋ DRURIDGE BAY, Northumberland ❋ PERRAN BEACH, Perranporth ❋ SLAPTON SANDS, Slapton

### Five British films about naturism in the 60s

*Travelling Light* ✻ *Nudist Paradise* ✻ *Forbidden Paradise* ✻ *As Nature Intended* ✻ *Shangri-la*

## THE NATURIST'S BIBLE

Although Britain isn't a major player on the international nudist scene in the way a country such as Germany is, it is from these shores that *Health & Efficiency Naturist* is published, a title that claims to be 'the world's only monthly commercial naturist magazine'. Originally a health and fitness mag when it launched in 1900, it went entirely nude in 1932.

### 20 rudest place names in Britain

BACK PASSAGE, City of London ◇ BEAVER CLOSE, Surrey ◇ BELL END, Birmingham ◇ COCK HEAD, North York Moors ◇ COCKS, Cornwall ◇ COCKSHOOT CLOSE, Oxfordshire ◇ DICK COURT, Lanarkshire ◇ FANNY AVENUE, Derbyshire ◇ FANNY HANDS LANE, Lincolnshire ◇ FINGRINGHOE, Essex ◇ HOLE OF HORCUM, North York Moors ◇ INCHINNAN DRIVE, Renfrewshire ◇ LICKFOLD, West Sussex ◇ MINGE LANE, Worcestershire ◇ MUFF, Northern Ireland ◇ SANDY BALLS, holiday centre in New Forest Hampshire ◇ SHITTERTON, Dorset ◇ SLAG LANE, Merseyside ◇ TURKEY COCK LANE, Colchester, Essex ◇ TWATT, Orkney and Shetland

Source: *Rude Britain: 100 Rudest Place Names in Britain* by Rob Bailey and Ed Hurst

### Gropec**t Lane

You may think the place names on page 177 are rude, but once upon a time Britain boasted several streets named 'Gropec**t Lane' in London, Bristol, Oxford, York and Newcastle. One theory is that the name, derived from the Middle Ages, was used to describe streets where prostitutes worked. They've all been renamed, mainly Grape Lane, although the one in London was changed to Grub Lane in the 18th century and then Milton Street in 1830, while the one in Oxford is now known as Magpie Lane.

## A SHORT HISTORY OF BRITISH NATURISM

Britain's first naturists didn't live in Britain at all, but in India, where a group of like-minded individuals formed the Fellowship of the Naked Trust in 1891. Its motto was *Vincat Natura* or 'Let Nature Win'. In 1922 Harold Booth set up the English Gymnosophist Society, headquartered in Wickford, Essex for those interested in 'nude life culture'. A few other clubs such as the Sun Bathing Society sprang up and then in 1943 the British Sun Bathing Association was formed to draw the disparate organizations under one umbrella. By the early 1950s it boasted 51 clubs as members, but then in 1954 a rival splinter group emerged, the Federation of British Sun Clubs. Against this backdrop of naked in-fighting, Britain's first naturist film, *Nudist Paradise*, was released in 1958. *The National Film Bulletin* describes it as inept, incompetent and 'its motives rather suspect'. The two rival groups came together in 1964 to form the Central Council for British Naturism, forerunner of today's British Naturism organization. By the 1970s cheap foreign travel meant British naturists began to go abroad. It was in 1979 – to a fair degree of shock and a great amount of tittering – that Britain's first official nudist beach opened in Brighton. Town councillor John Blackman described the beach as a 'flagrant exhibition of mammary glands'. Nonetheless, this beach remains nudist, and other British resorts have since joined it.

# NO SEX PLEASE, WE'RE BRITISH

*No Sex Please, We're British*, a farce about prudish Brits trying to deal with a mail-order mix up, when a newlywed couple receive a deluge of Scandinavian pornography, was first performed in London in 1971.

Though the critics groaned and slated Alistair Foot and Anthony Marriott's play, the public lapped it up, with the play running for nearly a decade. American audiences weren't so easily pleased. When it crossed the Atlantic, it lasted for just 16 performances. A film version starring Ronnie Corbett appeared in 1973.

> *Sexual intercourse began*
> *In nineteen sixty-three*
> *(Which was rather late for me)*
> *Between the end of the*
> *Chatterley ban*
> *And the Beatles' first LP.*
> First verse of Philip Larkin's poem,
> 'Annus Mirabilis'

 **In 2002 Ann Summers sold more than one million vibrators.**

---

## BRITISH SEX STATS

- *20% of people have sex before the age of 16, a fall from 32% in 2002.*
- *The average age at which women lose their virginity is 17.44 years, while for men it is 18.06.*
- *One in three women said they had had sex without their consent.*
- *14% of women said they had had non-consensual sex in order to keep the other person happy.*
- *Two-thirds of Britons believe that prostitution should be legalized.*
- *15% of Brits have had sexual contact with someone of the same sex.*
- *One in five Brits is dissatisfied with their sex life.*

Source: MORI poll commissioned by *The Observer* in 2006

In 2000, one in 23 British men had paid for sex according to *The National Survey of Sexual Attitudes and Lifestyles*

•

Britain is the world's fastest-growing market for Internet pornography according to a Neilsen Net ratings study in 2007

•

Homosexuality became legal in England and Wales in 1967, but strangely not until 1980 in Scotland

---

### The age of consent

❖The age of consent in Britain is 16, although in England and Wales it is illegal for a person in a position of trust, such as a doctor or a teacher, to engage in sexual activity with someone under the age of 18.

❖The age of consent was first set at 12 in Britain in 1275 and it wasn't until six centuries later in 1885 that it was raised to 16.

---

## PAGE THREE

Overseas visitors who regard the British as particularly prudish about sex and nudity are consistently shocked to open a copy of Britain's most popular newspaper, *The Sun*, to be greeted by a picture of a topless girl. The Page 3 girl was first introduced by Rupert Murdoch in 1969, but it wasn't until 17 November 1970, that the first model, Stephanie Rahn, appeared topless. The accompanying caption read:

*'We, like most of our readers, like pretty girls. And if they are as pretty as today's Birthday Suit girl, 20-year-old Stephanie Rahn, who cares whether they are dressed or not?'*

SOME FAMOUS PAGE 3 GIRLS: Leilani Dowding, Samantha Fox, Jo Guest, Jordan, Kathy Lloyd, Linda Lusardi, Melinda Messenger, Jayne Middlemiss, Lucy Pinder, Maria Whittaker.

## SAFE SEX

♦ The oldest condoms found in Britain dated back to 1640, when they were used to prevent the spread of venereal disease during the Civil War. The old-school sheaths were made from fish and animal intestines.

♦ The Pill, meanwhile, first became available in Britain in 1961 with an estimated 3.5 million women using it in 2003.

♦ Following a national 'sex quiz' in 2006, the Family Planning Association revealed that one in three people thinks vigorous exercise, visiting the bathroom or washing after sex ,will prevent pregnancy.

### Banned books:

The *Kama Sutra* was first translated into English by Sir Richard Burton in 1876, but remained illegal in Britain until 1963. D.H. Lawrence's novel *Lady Chatterley's Lover* was banned in Britain from 1927 until 1960 due to its 'raunchy' sexual descriptions.

## GOAT SEX

Back in 1533 Henry VIII passed a law against 'the abominable vice of buggery committed with man or beast', which was punishable by death until 1861. Nearly 500 years later Brits, it appeared, still hadn't learned their lesson. In 2002 passengers on the Hull to Bridlington service stared out of the train windows in amazement as they watched 23-year-old chef, Stephen Hall, bugger a goat in allotments near to his house. Apparently Hall had used his belt as a lasso to catch the goat. 'My friends have been giving me a lot of stick. I have never done anything like this before,' he said afterwards. He was sentenced to six months in prison.

# THE ROUTEMASTER BUS

Unveiled in 1954, the Routemaster bus is probably the most iconic bus in the world. Though you'd be hard pushed to find a more popular British image with overseas visitors, the distinctive double-decker buses are barely seen on the streets of London now. Withdrawal began in 1982, and by the 21st century they were all but phased out. Only two 'heritage' routes survive, served by bus numbers 9 and 15.

---

### Routemaster factoids

○ The last Routemaster was built in 1968. ○ *The Routemaster's double-act of driver and conductor was once described as 'the Lennon and McCartney of the road'.* ○ When Routemasters were at their peak, on average three people a year died while getting on or off the open platform. ○ *Routemaster conductor Duke Baysee used to play harmonica while collecting fares on the number 66.* ○ You can drive a Routemaster with an ordinary driving licence as long as you only carry eight passengers. ○ *'Bendy' buses, the replacements for Routemasters on many routes, can carry 140 passengers (admittedly in cattle truck conditions), while most Routemasters had seating for 72 – those without a seat could only stand on the lower deck.*

---

## THE DATES ON WHICH THE ROUTEMASTER DIED

The following 20 bus routes stopped being served by Routemasters on the following dates:

**11:** *31 October 2003* ◇ **23:** *14 November 2003* ◇ **94:** *23 January 2004* ◇ **6:** *26 March 2004* ◇ **98:** *26 March 2004* ◇ **8:** *4 June 2004* ◇ **7:** *2 July 2004* ◇ **137:** *9 July 2004* ◇ **390:** *3 September 2004* ◇ **73:** *3 September 2004* ◇ **12:** *5 November 2004* ◇ **36:** *28 January 2005* ◇ **19:** *1 April 2005* ◇ **14:** *22 July 2005* ◇ **22:** *22 July 2005* ◇ **13:** *21 October 2005* ◇ **38:** *28 October 2005* ◇ **159:** *9 December 2005*

# GOING UNDERGROUND

Comprising 274 stations and over 253 miles of track the London Underground is the world's oldest underground system and represents the bedrock and bane of many a working Londoner's life. Busier and more expensive than its European counterparts, the Tube seems to be one place where people forget the innate British tendency to queue and, instead, barge, bustle and bark like a pack of starving hyenas, threatening to rip each other apart in an effort to board trains ... every day!!

| NAME | MAP COLOUR | FIRST SECTION | STATIONS |
|------|-----------|---------------|----------|
| Bakerloo Line | Brown | 1906 | 25 |
| Central Line | Red | 1900 | 49 |
| Circle Line | Yellow | 1884 | 27 |
| District Line | Green | 1868 | 60 |
| East London Line | Orange | 1869 | 8 |
| Hammersmith & City Line | Pink | 1863 | 28 |
| Jubilee Line | Silver | 1979 | 27 |
| Metropolitan Line | Magenta | 1863 | 34 |
| Northern Line | Black | 1890 | 50 |
| Piccadilly Line | Dark Blue | 1906 | 52 |
| Victoria Line | Light Blue | 1968 | 16 |
| Waterloo & City Line | Teal | 1898 | 2 |

 In 1911, a wooden-legged man known as 'Bumper' Harris was employed to ride the first-ever Underground escalator at Earl's Court to demonstrate how safe it was.

# WEIRD BRITAIN

*'We got sucked up by politics and that's what we weren't about: we were about politics but not about politics if that makes sense.'*
Dangerous Dave, Monster Raving Loony Party

## THE MONSTER RAVING LOONY PARTY

Howling Laud Hope, Dangerous Dave, Lord Toby Jug, Mr R.U. Serious and The Flying Pastie sound more like members of the Bash Street Kids or joke DJs than politicians, but all have stood in national elections and the Monster Raving Loony Party has succeeded in making itself part of the British political tradition. Its late leader, Screaming Lord Sutch, who used to drive around in a Rolls-Royce emblazoned with a Union Jack, set up the first incarnation of the party in 1964 and committed suicide in 1999. Sutch fought and lost more elections than anybody else in British political history and was the UK's longest-serving party leader.

The party's policies are unorthodox: joggers should be made to run on giant treadmills that generate electricity for public use; all bald people must wear hats; anyone using a mobile phone in a cinema has to be squirted with silly string; and Britain should be towed 500 miles south to improve the climate. But Loonies argue that it's only a matter of time before the mainstream political parties adopt their ideas. After all they originally campaigned for the vote at 18, pet passports and for pubs to open all day.

The party has also enjoyed some modest electoral success. In the early 1990s, 16 councillors associated with the Monster Raving Loony Party were elected, while Howling Laud Hope and Chris 'Screwy' Driver became mayors. Loonys aren't as united as they used to be, however. In the early 21st century, the movement suffered a political schism, splitting into two entities – the Official Monster Raving Loony Party and the Rock 'N' Roll Loony Party.

## THE WEIRDEST TOWN IN BRITAIN

Llanwrtyd Wells in Wales may not be the smallest town in Britain as it claims (that title belongs to Fordwich, Kent), but it is almost certainly the weirdest. On New Year's Eve people roam around town brandishing torches, following a horse's skull nailed to a stick. Come summer and it hosts a Morris dancers dance-off, the World Mountain Bike Bog Snorkelling Championships and the annual Man vs Horse race, a gruelling 22-mile cross-country marathon in which runners attempt to beat men riding horses. For the rest of the year locals amuse themselves with competitive rambles and beer festivals. The town is also home to 'Rob the Rubbish'. Robin Kevan, as he was born, is famous for his efforts to clean up the British countryside and spends his days striding around Britain picking up litter on a one-man crusade against rubbish.

### The Handlebar Moustache Club

On every first Friday of the month a group of men with a truly impressive array of facial hair gather around a pub table in The Windsor Castle, west London. They all sport handlebar moustaches, but the variety of styles is enormous. Some look like walruses after electro-shock therapy, while others look like their facial fuzz has been hardened into sharp points with concrete. The Handlebar Moustache Club has been meeting to smoke pipes, compare tweeds and discuss facial hair over a pint for the last 19 years, but as an institution it has existed since 1947. Anyone can join the club as long as they have, as 66-year-old club president Ted Sedman puts it: 'A hirsute appendage of the upper lip with graspable extremities.' In other words you have to possess a moustache that is so big you can comfortably yank either end of it. Beards, naturally, are banned.

The Handlebar Moustache Club has an annual darts match in April against the Pipe Smokers Club.

## THE BURRY MAN

Every year on the second Friday an eerie, green mannequin that wouldn't look out of place in a schlock horror B-movie walks the streets of South Queensferry in Edinburgh. Human eyes peer forth from plant-rimmed sockets, but every other body part is smothered with vegetation. The figure sports a floral hat, burrs and ferns adorn its entire body and a rose springs forth from each nipple.

It's not a swamp monster, nor is it a trick of the light; it's not even a performance artist from London who's taken the wrong turning out of the Edinburgh Festival. No, it's a centuries-old Scottish custom known as the Burry Man, whereby a South Queensferry townsman completely covers his body in sticky seeds known as burrs and parades across town calling in at numerous houses, pubs and places of work.

He follows a seven-mile route around town and at each venue he accepts a dram of whisky which he drinks through a straw. He has two staves and is followed by two attendants who become increasingly useful as his ten-hour day wears on and the whisky weighs ever heavier in his veins.

Exactly what the Burry Man represents is unclear. Some say he's a Celtic fertility God, while others equate him with The Green Man figure that appears frequently in British folklore. A popular local theory is that the Burry Man is a scapegoat figure employed to cleanse the town of evil spirits. In ancient times the ceremony would have ended with a ritual killing but these days the only thing that seems in danger of sacrifice is his liver.

## THE COLONY THAT NEVER WAS

Would you buy land rights in Latin America from a Scotsman called Gregor MacGregor who claimed to be the cazique of the Principality of Poyais? Never mind Poyais, even the  name Gregor MacGregor sounds made up. Nonetheless, plenty of people invested in the 'fertile', 'untapped' land of Poyais where MacGregor claimed there was already a small colony of British settlers who had founded the capital, St Joseph. Poyais, naturally, was free of the tropical disease that plagued other colonies in Central America. In September 1822, the *Honduras Packet* set sail from London carrying 70 settlers and then four months later another ship, *The Kennersley Castle*, left Leith with another 200 settlers aboard. The first ship was also carrying Poyais dollars, a currency MacGregor had printed in Scotland. When they arrived, they found untouched jungle, a few natives and a couple of American hermits. Poyais it was quite clear did not exist. Eventually, around 50 of the would-be settlers made it back to Britain, but by the time the story was published in British newspapers, MacGregor was nowhere to be found. He'd moved to Paris where he was busy selling the Republic of Poyais to gullible French.

### WEIRD CONTESTS

JUNE ✦ World Toe Wrestling Championship ✦ *Derbyshire* JUNE ✦ World Stinging Nettle Eating Championship ✦ *Dorset* JULY ✦ Shin Kicking Championship ✦ *Gloucestershire* JULY ✦ World Pea Shooting Championship ✦ *Cambridgeshire* AUGUST ✦ Mobile Phone Throwing Championship ✦ *London* SEPTEMBER ✦ World Black Pudding Throwing Championship ✦ Lancashire

## SHROVETIDE FOOTBALL

If you don't believe that British men in the provinces spend a lot of their time fighting in car parks, then it's worth paying a visit to Ashbourne in Derbyshire on Shrove Tuesday. Marauding violently across the town will be a roaring brawl, a literally 'steaming' mess of flailing limbs, shaved heads, red faces and rugby tops. Nominally, the several hundred men involved in the mayhem are taking part in the ancient tradition of Shrovetide football, but it tends to be difficult to see the ball and the main involvement of feet appears to be the collision between steel toe-capped boots and various body parts.

Part-football-part-fight, part-rugby-part-riot, the game of Shrovetide football dates back over 800 years. Played on a pitch that's three miles long and two miles wide, featuring the picturesque market town of Ashbourne slap bang in the middle, the game has virtually no rules. You're not allowed to murder anybody or commit manslaughter, and it's forbidden to transport the ball via motor vehicle, but other than that anything goes. Hundreds of players make up the two teams and locals play for the Up'ards or the Down'ards depending on whether they were born north or south of the river that runs through Ashbourne.

---

### David Icke

Calling David Icke eccentric is a bit like saying Hitler liked dogs: it's probably true, but misses the point. Yes, David Icke is an eccentric, but he's also quite probably insane. As an ex-Coventry City goalkeeper he's an unlikely 'son of God', but this is what he told the British public he was in a TV interview with Terry Wogan in 1991. Icke is also convinced the world is run by a race of reptilian humanoids, known as the Babylonian Brotherhood, including among others the Queen Mother, George Bush, Tony Blair and the late US country singer, Boxcar Willie. Strange man. What's perhaps not so strange is that he no longer lives in Britain, but in the US where he has found a more receptive audience for his beliefs.

---

## The most extreme race in the world

Pits of fire, electric fences, barbed wire, muddy swamps, freezing water, and hidden ditches are just some of the obstacles in the annual Tough Guy race, which combines a seven-mile cross-country run with an intimidating, some would say insane, assault course. People travel from all over the world to compete in the contest, which Billy Wilson has held on his farm since 1987. He used to fire live bullets above contestants, but Health & Safety banned this practice. Injuries are common and one year six broken legs led Wilson to announce over the PA system that there would be a prize for the seventh. One person has died at the event, Michael Green, who had a faulty heart valve and completed the race only to collapse with a heart attack in his wife's arms.

## COAL CARRYING

Many strange ideas and bizarre bets are conceived by two men in a pub. Few result in international competitions, but that's exactly how the World Coal Carrying Competition, held annually in the Yorkshire village of Gawthorpe, came about. Back in 1963, coal merchant Lewis Hartley wandered into his local, the Beehive Inn. He spotted a friend, Reggie Sedgewick, and slapping him on the back, Hartley uttered the immortal words, 'Ba gum, lad, tha' looks buggered!' Sedgewick took offence at this slight against his manhood and, spluttering into his bitter, challenged Hartley to an endurance race to settle who was the fittest. Being deep in coal country and even deeper into a drinking session, they decided they should race with sacks of coal strapped to their backs: £10 was wagered, a date set for Easter Monday and from such inauspicious and alcohol-riddled origins an internationally recognized event was born. One entrant describes it as 'the most pain I've ever felt in any single event. I had backache for about six weeks afterwards.'

## CHEESE ROLLING

A cheese hurtles downhill at high speed. In pursuit are 20 grown men, careering, crashing and turning somersaults down an incline that could double as a ski slope. Within 15 seconds one man knocks himself unconscious, another's ankle bone pops out at a right angle, a spectator faints and the race is over. Stretcher-bearers move in, the winner receives the 7lb cheese and the crowd readies itself for the next race. Four of these suicide runs are held in a single afternoon each year on Cooper's Hill in Brockworth, Gloucestershire. Locals began flinging their bodies down a steep slope after a lump of dairy produce hundreds of years ago. You can tell how dangerous the event is by the fact that the organization hired to retrieve the injured is SARAID, a firm that normally deals with the after-effects of earthquakes, avalanches and other emergencies.

### Aleister Crowley

Once described as the 'wickedest man in the world' for dabbling with Satanism, Aleister Crowley was born into an evangelical Christian household in Leamington Spa in 1875 and went to Cambridge University, before dedicating his life to the occult. Crowley was obsessed with the darker side of mysticism. He was also a drug addict and a bisexual at a time when admitting to such marked you out as a degenerate, but he was also a painter and a poet and a keen mountain climber and chess player. He was also, quite possibly, insane – he did after all name his first daughter, Nuit Ma Ahathoor Hecate Sappho Jezebel Lilith Crowley. He became a celebrity and founded his own religion, Thelema, setting up a sort of anti-church in Sicily, the Abbey of Theleme, where he and his followers indulged in sexual rituals and other ceremonies, before Mussolini booted him out of the country. He died penniless and addicted to heroin in a boarding house in Hastings in 1947 at the age of 72.

# AULD LANG SYNE

'Auld Lang Syne' is the song people in Britain sing at the stroke of midnight on New Year's Eve. Based on a poem by Scottish poet, Robert Burns, it's not entirely clear why the singing of the song has become such a firm New Year's tradition in Britain. Few people know all the lyrics to the first verse and chorus and tend to drunkenly hum, mumble and make up the words to these without ever tackling the other verses, which are printed here:

## AULD LANG SYNE

*Should auld acquaintance be forgot,*
*and never brought to mind?*
*Should auld acquaintance be forgot,*
*and auld lang syne?*

*CHORUS:*
*For auld lang syne, my dear,*
*for auld lang syne,*
*we'll take a cup o' kindness yet,*
*for auld lang syne.*

*OTHER VERSES*
*And surely you'll buy your pint cup!*
*And surely I'll buy mine!*
*And we'll take a cup o' kindness yet,*
*for auld lang syne.*

*We two have run about the hills,*
*and pulled the daisies fine ;*
*But we've wandered many a weary foot,*
*since auld lang syne.*

*We two have paddled in the stream,*
*from morning sun till dine (dinner time) ;*
*But seas between us broad have roared*
*since auld lang syne.*

*And there's a hand my trusty friend!*
*And give us a hand o' thine!*
*And we'll take a right good-will*
*draught,*
*for auld lang syne.*

# FAMOUS LAST WORDS

*'I am not the least afraid to die.'*
Charles Darwin (1809–1882)

✳

*'Am I dying or is this my birthday?'*
Lady Nancy Astor (1879–1964)
who was the first female
Member of Parliament

✳

*'No.'*
Alexander Graham Bell (1847–1922)

✳

*'Bury me where my arrow falls…'*
Robin Hood

✳

*'I am just going outside and may be
some time.'*
Captain Lawrence Oates (1880–1912)
on the ill-fated expedition to the South
Pole in 1911–12

✳

*'Oh God, have pity on my soul. Oh
God, have pity on my soul.'*
Anne Boleyn (c. 1507–1536)

✳

*'Why not? After all, it belongs to him.'*
Charlie Chaplin (1889–1977)

✳

*'Are you sure it's safe?'*
Murderer Dr William Palmer
(1824–1856) as he looked at the
trapdoor above the gallows

*'Go away. I'm all right.'*
H.G. Wells (1866–1946)

✳

*'My design is to make what haste
I can to be gone.'*
Oliver Cromwell (1599–1658)

✳

*'My God. What's happened?'*
Princess Diana (1961–1997)

✳

*'Bugger Bognor.'*
King George V (1865–1936)

✳

*'Good night.'*
Lord Byron (1788–1824)

✳

*'Dying is easy. Comedy is difficult.'*
English stage actor Edmund Gwenn
(1875–1959)

✳

*'Strike, man, strike!'*
Sir Walter Raleigh (c. 1554–1618)

✳

*'God bless you, Hardy.'*
Vice Admiral Horatio Nelson
(1758–1805)

✳

*'All my possessions for a moment
of time.'*
Elizabeth I, Queen of England
(1533–1603)